Time Off for Good Behavior

How Hardworking Women Can

Take a Break and Change Their Lives

Mary Lou Quinlan

Mary Lou

BROADWAY BOOKS

New York

TIME OFF FOR GOOD BEHAVIOR

HOW HARDWORKING WOMEN CAN TAKE A BREAK AND CHANGE THEIR LIVES

Copyright © 2005 by Mary Lou Quinlan.

Broadway Books titles may be purchased for business or promotional use or for special sales. For information, please write to: Special Markets Department, Random House, Broadway Books, specialmarkets@randomhouse.com

PRINTED IN THE UNITED STATES OF AMERICA

BROADWAY BOOKS and its logo, a letter B bisected on the diagonal, are trademarks of Random House, Inc.

Visit our website at www.broadwaybooks.com

First edition published 2005

Book design by Nicola Fergusen

Library of Congress Cataloging-in-Publication Data

Quinlan, Mary Lou.
Time off for good behavior : how hardworking women can take a break and change their lives / Mary Lou Quinlan.
p. cm.
Includes bibliographical references.
Contents: Why I wrote this book—The women "before"; My story; Growing up good; Working hard, feeling the burn; Your money or your life; The moment of truth; What time off feels like; After time off; The women "after"; A postscript to America's companies.
ISBN 0-7679-1831-2
1. Women executives—Job stress—United States.
2. Businesswomen—Job stress—United States. 3. Women—Job stress—United States.
4. Women—Employment—United States.
5. Burn out (Psychology)—United States. 6. Self-actualization (Psychology)
I. Title: Working women can take a break and change their lives. II. Title.

HD6054.4.U6Q85 2005
158.7'23'082—dc22   2004054532

1 3 5 7 9 10 8 6 4 2

With love and thanks to Joe,
who always kept the light on for me

ACKNOWLEDGMENTS

I wanted to write this story the minute that I ended my own time off in 1998. I tried. But I learned that the true benefits of time off take time to reveal themselves. And I wanted to spend some time walking the walk before declaring victory as a "time-off" rookie.

With the distance and perspective of six years, I've also realized how many people in my life contributed to my journey before and after time off. And that's who I want to thank.

For being the first good girl role models in my life, I thank the Sisters of St. Joseph from St. Helena's School in Philadelphia. As women working for love, not money, they win the Olympics of good behavior. To my teachers at Cardinal Dougherty High School and Saint Joseph's University, my appreciation for giving me the confidence to live life as I have.

Like the women in this book, the first words of encouragement that stay with you for a lifetime come from our parents. There aren't two people in the world who have been more loyal and loving than my mom and dad, Mary and Ray Finlayson. With my brother Jack, my trusted friend and role model, they are the cheering section of my life and I love and thank them.

There are many women in my life and in this book who deserve special recognition. The thirty-seven women who shared their stories, and the coaches and psychologists and corporate leaders who shared their experiences made this book a joy to write. I am indebted to the women of Just Ask a Woman, Cara Pontillo, Jen Drechsler, and Tracy Chapman, whose wisdom and patience anchored me in what women really think and want. And a special thank-you to Barrie Dolnick and Susan Lemak, who believed in this book from the beginning.

Reaching out and listening to dozens of women takes a team. Liz Gerst worked with me on the early investigation, linking me to many of the terrific women inside. And Suzanne Allard Levingston, the archetype Type A good girl, was a heaven-sent contributor, with her careful research, honest feedback, and sharp investigative skills.

Finally, the women of Broadway Books, my editor Trish Medved and assistant editor Beth Datlowe. Trish's leadership, insights, and humor kept me from overindexing on my Type A-ness, most of the time.

Behind a happy woman, you'll often find a wonderful man. There are a few I'd like to thank—my terrific agent, Wes Neff, stress expert Dr. Redford Williams from the book, and the man who set me free to take this time off, my former boss and forever friend, Roy Bostock.

The last two males in my life are Danny Boy and Joe. My dog Danny slept at my feet, page after page, to show that he totally "gets" the joy of time off. And to my rock, the guy who's believed in me since the day we met in 1976 and who makes me feel proud to say, "I'm Joe's wife"—Joe Quinlan. No one could ask for a better partner or love.

CONTENTS

Time Off for
Good Behavior

INTRODUCTION
WHY I WROTE THIS BOOK

Have you ever fantasized about taking real time off? Can you picture what it would be like to wake up at your own pace, spend the day doing whatever you wanted to do, and sleep all the way through the night? Can you imagine a weekend, a month, even a year as a rest stop during a lifetime of working so hard?

I set out to write this book because I had a revelation: With a little time off, not only can you get a much needed break, you can change your life. It took me years of working like a lunatic to learn this simple truth.

For me, time off was always "someday." "Someday, I'll get away..." "If I could just get a few days to myself..." My dreams always ended in "dot, dot, dot," since I never believed I could do it. I talked about it. I wished for it. But I just kept working hard, because I loved what I did and "the next big thing" kept me from taking any action. It wasn't until I burned out that I walked away.

You may be living this story or you may be heading down this same path and not even realize it. When you're working really hard, it's difficult to see how stressed you are and even harder to let go. I admit that while writing this book about taking time off, I found myself getting stressed about deadlines and compulsively overworking all over again. When we're chasing our goals, we try so hard to stick it out that we don't even notice that we're stuck.

I listen to women on behalf of corporations for a living, and I eavesdrop on women's conversations all the time. Here's what I often overhear: "My day starts at six and doesn't end till I crash into bed after midnight...I've got to get a break or I'll die." "I don't know how much longer I can go at this pace...the kids, the job, where's my life?" "I'm working like crazy and there's no letting up... is this all there is?" As hardworking women, we commiserate and we worry and we complain, but too often we don't stop to recognize that the only person who can call a halt to an overworked and under-rested life is facing us in the mirror.

The value of listening to yourself and taking some action is that you can discover that time off will give you the chance to see what is really important in your life. When you give yourself permission to take some time off for your good behavior, you will see that it is possible to create a life that is aligned with your passions. You will experience what many women have already learned. Time off can be the escape valve that reenergizes you and helps you reimagine the life you want to lead and the work you want to do.

It begins with understanding how you got to be so overworked in the first place.

Type A Poster Child

I grew up as a Type A good girl who believed that doing my best was the least I could do. Jump? How high? It's due Thursday? Would it be better for you if I finished it Wednesday instead? That dedication stuck with me throughout my career, and it propelled me to the top job at a big company. But when I hit my forties, I hit a wall. After twenty-three years of saying "yes" to every opportunity, every late-night meeting, every request from above and below, I finally said the two words I had never said in my life: "I quit."

Actually, I didn't quit at first. I made a career move unheard of for a busy working woman. I took time off. I didn't sail around the world or join an ashram. I spent five weeks, mostly at home, getting my life back. I've since been told that five weeks doesn't even count. When I referred to it as a sabbatical, people laughed. But, as anyone who's ever been engulfed in work fever knows, five weeks is a lifetime.

I hoped that during my time off I would simply rest and start breathing again. I did. The big surprise to me was how much clearer my thinking was once I let myself off the hook. In the office, each day had been a relentless race to please everyone and do everything. Once I was on the outside, I saw my driven life in clear relief. I was able to refocus my priorities on what really mattered, rather than just on what had to be done.

Thanks to that life raft of a little space, I opened my mind to a new career and a new perspective. More importantly, I rediscovered the woman I had lost long ago on the upward climb.

The benefits of taking time are big and small. Since my leave in 1998, I've created a new company based on my talents, and have developed a new career as a writer, speaker, and motivator for women. But it's the little things that I discovered that I treasure, like sleeping at night, walking my dog, enjoying a second cup of coffee, and hanging out with friends. This experience has been so liberating, I decided to go public. Here's why.

Unmasking the Myth

As working women, we may hold an idealized vision of success. We grew up hoping to be the chick in the great suit. She may be in the corner office or on the magazine cover or in the operating room or wherever, but she's successful and she's loving it. Ideally, our career girl is also the perfect wife to her fabulous husband and the perfect mother to her well-adjusted kids. Or she's the cool woman-about-town who's single and ambitious, running from the boardroom to the nightclub. She's always on and she's not showing the strain *outside.*

The real story isn't so pretty. Inside, our heroine is exhausted, and though she may love what she does, her resilience is wearing thin. She needs a break, big time. Unfortunately, it's not coming soon, not if anyone else in her life has anything to say about it. Her peers are amazed at all she can do. Her boss expects her to keep on performing. Her associates depend on her. And she certainly doesn't want to disappoint her family, who are so proud of her, need her income, admire her stamina, and bask in the glow of her achievements.

If you crave a break, you're not alone. According to a recent national poll, almost seven in ten people who make $40,000 or more a year fantasize about taking at least several months off, and one in five thirty-five to forty-nine-year-olds fantasizes about it daily.[1]

I know that there are women who say, "I want to, but I just can't do it." They worry about money and family needs; they just can't deal with it now; they have an overwhelming fear of honestly facing their future. One of the biggest barriers is not knowing what comes next: What if I take some time and nothing changes? they think, or, What if my situation just gets worse?

Consider the alternative. What if I told you that six months or a year from now, you would still be doing the exact same thing, day after day? How does that make you feel? If you feel like you are suffocating slowly, then it's time to do something about it.

My counsel to the "I can'ts" is to recognize that, if we are lucky or blessed, we have dozens of working years before us. Over the course of a career that could last ten or twenty or thirty or even forty more years, isn't there one month that you could claim as your own? Or seven days out of the 16,060 days of your life between age twenty-one and sixty-five?

The truth is, as Americans, we are working more hours a week than ever before. A study from the New York–based Families and Work Institute revealed that "combined weekly work hours for dual-earning couples with children rose ten hours per week, from eighty-one hours in 1977 to ninety-one hours in 2002."[2] Meanwhile, we don't even take the vacation we've earned. According to a 2003 survey by Expedia.com, employees are handing their companies back $21 billion in unused vacation days. We're not even taking time when we're paid to do it.[3]

What's the result of all this overwork? Stress. And ironically, this stress from overwork drives us away from our jobs. Forty percent of job turnover is due to stress. An estimated one million workers are absent each day because of stress. And stress costs businesses a lot of money. According to the American Institute of Stress website (yes, there really is such a thing!), "Job stress is also very costly, with the price tag for U.S. industry estimated at over $300 billion annually as a result of accidents, absenteeism, employee turnover, diminished productivity, direct medical, legal and insurance costs, workers' compensation awards, as well as tort and FELA judgments."[4]

Enough Is Enough

When I first set out to tell my story, I wondered if I were violating a secret code of silence. Women who make it believe they are expected to carry the flag for all women. As a group, we've worked so hard that when we achieve money, titles, and responsibility, we feel like we owe it to the others to stick it out, stress and all.

Even beyond my betrayal of the female success myth, was I breaking the good girl rules I'd grown up believing? I was raised to think that if things got tough, I needed to put one foot in front of the other and keep on going. It was clear that working hard was a requirement and that being a good girl was the rule.

My seventy-nine-year-old father-in-law, who's always been supportive of my career, asked me what this book was about. When I told him, he looked at me skeptically and said, "I don't get it. Wasn't the whole idea that women wanted to get these great jobs and be successful? Now you're telling me that they want to get out of them and take time off?"

Not all of us do. But over the past several years, I have met many women who are saying, "Enough is enough." Even the most buttoned-up female clients of my consulting business have pulled me aside to ask, "Can I talk to you about doing what you did?" They are searching for an escape hatch, or at least a way to get their mojo back. As I shared my story, I found a swelling underground of women, hungry with questions: How did you do it? Weren't you scared? What did you do when you were off? What do you do now? Do you miss your old job? Do you ever regret it? How can I do it?

This is a book for women who are worn down from trying so hard and caring so much. The first women to identify with my story were women in their late thirties and their early forties. Many women post thirty-five have begun to wonder: Is this all there is? Whether it's the shock of the "big" birthdays or the frustration of having worked fifteen years, with another twenty-five to go, a deep restlessness forces women to look in the mirror and face the rest of their lives. Many of these women, especially the moms, are angry or tired, or just plain desperate for an "out."

As I opened up, I met women of all different life stages who were feeling what I felt. Women in their fifties and sixties responded to my story because they yearned to realize dreams that had been buried too long. Their fires still burned to get it right before their careers and lives were summed up by "what might have been."

I connected with women in their early thirties, many of whom shot out of college to become the first generation of high-earning "whippersnappers" who got lured into the big money and titles and "forgot" to build a personal life. Once they moved into maturity and marriage or motherhood, they realized how much they'd neglected the life part of the elusive work/life balance equation.

When I was starting my career, I remember that my peers and I were hellbent on getting ahead. We figured that our personal lives would eventually and magically fall into place, once we'd "made it." I remember my female colleagues in the eighties who used to have maternity leave races: Who could work till the last minute, have the baby, and get back to the job the fastest?

Thankfully, today's young women take a different approach. From the start of their working years, women in their twenties are more forthcoming and determined about their expectations to have both a fulfilling career *and* a happy life, not one or the other. I believe that growing up as the daughters of stressed working mothers made many of them worry about making that kind of personal sacrifice in their own lives. As one twenty-four-year-old daughter of a working mother said to me, "When I was growing up, I just wanted to grab my mother by the shoulder pads and scream, 'Why can't you be like the other moms and stay home with me and wear a sweatsuit?' "

These young women are more vocal about their intentions to seek balance in their lives, and even take time off during their careers. Statistics bear this out. According to a 2001 survey by Catalyst, 61 percent of Generation Xers either are taking or wanting to take sabbaticals.[5]

I am also writing this for the future generations of working women. I have spoken to high school and college-age women about burning out. Even the most career-fixated MBAs at Ivy Leagues register shock and fear at the prospect of a job that can swallow their identity. They consistently ask me, "Is it possible to have a career and still have a life?"

I want all women—all the Type A good girls and those who are in training—to know that they can work hard and succeed. But they can also take a break. By thinking holistically about what they might want in their jobs and their lives, they can write a new story of what it means to have a life that's both professionally and personally satisfying.

How This Book Will Work for You

Time Off for Good Behavior is a commonsense book about something too uncommon, relief from our get-ahead world. I will examine how we get to be so driven in the first place, and how we unconsciously succumb to the 24/7 culture of overwork that feeds our desires to please and overachieve. I'll advocate for the simple value of giving yourself permission to rest, to help you put some space in your life to think, to breathe, to nap, to be.

I am not a psychologist. I'm a woman who lived this story and still struggles to get it right. In writing this book, I reached out to a number of experts, life coaches, counselors, and therapists who added their experienced analysis to what I heard from the women who lived it. I also talked with some enlightened companies who hold the keys to setting us free. While we have a long way to go to get to a more human and livable workplace, there are a few corporate beacons that might lead us to a new collective attitude toward the importance of flexibility during our working years.

I'll tell my story, and also include stories from dozens of other women I met who had "yes-ed" their way into a wall. I tripped onto a live geyser of women bursting to spread the word of their time-off revelations. For this book, I focused on thirty-seven remarkable women who stopped punching the clock—just for a while.

You'll meet Lisa, a thirty-six-year-old executive in the travel industry who worked so hard, she managed to nearly lose her friends and kill a budding romance. Only a startling moment of truth jolted her out of her out-of-control life. I'll tell the story of Courtney, thirty-three, who went from Internet queen to bankrupt divorcee in one year, and found that time off was the only medicine that healed. And you'll meet Donna G., forty-four, who is still working manically and craving the time off that she's afraid to take.

Some of the women leapt with no plan, while others strategized their leave for years. You'll hear from moms, like Leslie, who at twenty-six suddenly quit when faced with a very sick child, and Jane, forty-six, who planned her sabbatical with her daughter for four years. Women in this book used their time off to go back to school, to start a new business, to travel the world, or simply to lie on the beach. All of them awakened to a new sense of themselves. Most of them are back at work, some at their same job, more often at new ones. Others are still searching.

These women of various life stages and professions, married and singles, moms and not, women in their thirties, forties, and fifties, from seventeen cities and towns across the country, from New York to Dallas to Sante Fe, will share their fears, their advice, their victories, and their lessons learned. You will hear their voices as they explore their first ambitions, their expanding agendas, the "A-ha" moments that led to the realizations that they really needed time off—and the stories of what they did and how they changed. The examples of their career transformations are amazing, but their internal changes are even more inspiring. They all learned that taking time off isn't an end in itself (although for many, it can become addictive). It's a catapult toward what's next.

To support you in your own "what's next?" decisions, I've included exercises at the end of each chapter. These simple questions can help you take a look at your own hardworking life, your goals and concerns, and even offer ways to figure out what emotional and financial considerations you'll need to make to take your own time off.

What Does "Time Off" Mean?

When you first hear "time off," you may think I mean a long, drawn-out sabbatical. Or months painting on a mountaintop. No. In this book, time off means time claimed as your own. Not a family vacation. Not a business trip. Time where *your* agenda is the only agenda. Some women got it the way I did, by stretching owed vacation. Others quit and took their chances. Some were fired or laid off, but instead of running to the next wrong job, they took time to regroup and recharge. Some lucky women took advantage of company-sponsored breaks. Maternity leaves grew to time off when women decided that the allotted time wasn't enough. Some used the time to reconnect with family or to resurrect a hidden talent.

Sometimes the saddest of circumstances, like the discovery of breast cancer or a mother's death, led to soul-searching and change. Some women have even taken multiple time offs throughout their careers, as preventive medicine for job boredom or to expand their options.

Despite my passion for the value of time off, I won't suggest that a woman quit when she is the sole support of a family, without sufficient resources to make ends meet. She may desperately want to, but the pressures for income are too overwhelming to indulge even a needed fantasy. Fortunately, as you'll hear from a few of the moms on their own, there is hope when there's a plan, especially a financial one. Time off can become an option for your life no matter what your circumstances are. (Just taking the vacation you're given is a start!)

How long is time off? As long as it takes to let off steam and let in enough oxygen so you can breathe again. I intentionally don't use the word "sabbatical." It's loaded with too much freight, and it might scare you into thinking, I can't do that.

One woman I interviewed re-thought her career in an afternoon, another in a week on a beach, another through twenty-five years of journal keeping. This book is not a formulaic prescription for course-correcting a career or a life. It is a collection of personal advice and professional suggestions for how to take a break so that you can retain the energy and passion for further success and satisfaction.

Not for Women Only, But . . .

I've been asked, "Why is this book for women?" As in, what about men? Certainly, men need and deserve a break and many will read this book and decide to take some time off. Younger men are particularly open to this idea. But I wrote it for women for several reasons. First, I listen to women every day at my company, Just Ask a Woman, a strategic marketing company that helps corporations understand their female customers. After interviewing thousands of them I understand their motivations and reasons for postponing time off. Secondly, women are still the primary caretakers of children, which compounds the stress of their jobs and intensifies their need for relief. Also, as natural sharers, women are more willing to admit when they are burning out. Personal happiness is at least as important to them as career success. They don't tie their identities to their jobs as often as men do. But, though it's not written specifically for them, if men take this message to heart as well, that's good news for everyone.

Why You Shouldn't Be Afraid If Your Employees Are Reading This . . .

I hope that the corporate leaders and business owners who read this book take it for what it is: a real-world look at the psychology of their best workers.

As a former CEO of a large company, I know how difficult it is to attract and retain the best people. With the impending glacial retirement of the baby boomers, we are facing an unprecedented labor shortage. Retention is fast becoming a critical priority in our country.[6] The women I interviewed and their good girl counterparts around the country are the employees that every company wants. They're often the hardest workers, the ones who excel and care, the ones they count on. Knowing what's going on in their minds can help businesses watch out and prepare for the signs of wearing out.

Better yet, this awareness can help businesses anticipate and respond to women's needs for a reprieve, whether with formal flexible schedules and paid leaves, or à la carte time rewards for the most talented and industrious workers. This is a timely issue because, like it or not, many of these women are one step short of the door. A total of 52 percent of the respondents to a national Harris survey by recruiting firm Spherion indicated a desire to change jobs, with 75 percent of those respondents seeking a change within the next year.[7] The burnout rate of the hardest-working women may or may not be the fault of corporate America, but it is their problem, and it's to their advantage if they solve it. Time off is not the only answer. But it beats getting the bad news that a valued woman is leaving because she needs a break and thinks she can't get it from you.

Before It's Too Late

One lesson I'll share at the start. At the end of my personal retreat, I wrote a list of what I loved and hated to do. It turned out to be a road map of what I ought to be doing with my life. My list made it clear that I needed to leave my high-profile job for something I could give my heart to. As I was packing up my desk from the job I quit in late 1998, I came across two other pieces of paper. Remarkably, each was nearly identical to the list I had just written. Unfortunately, I had written one list on the stationery of my 1994 job and the other was dated 1988. In other words, I had been thinking of this escape to a new life as long as ten years before. It took me a decade to listen to my own voice. My hope is that this book will encourage you not to wait as long as I did.

Don't wait too long. You have probably heard stories about women who have. Two years ago, I had lunch with a very successful female colleague. A forty-nine-year-old mom of three and the "office mom" of several hundred employees, she confided in me that since her boys were approaching their last years of high school and her daughter was turning ten, she would love to take some time so she could be with them for these important years. She had worked for twenty-five years without a real break and she talked about how great it would feel to have some time to just be herself and not a boss. "But not yet," she said, "maybe next year." Two weeks after her fiftieth birthday, my friend died from a brain aneurism. Next year never came.

If there's one thing that women deserve and demand, it's honesty. We've had too many years of buying into the success myths. We've perpetuated them ourselves. We keep up the secret handshake that says it's inappropriate to get this far and then say, "Enough." But it's time for an alternative story to be told.

PROLOGUE
THE WOMEN OF <u>TIME OFF FOR GOOD BEHAVIOR</u>—"BEFORE"

A s I gathered the stories of nearly forty women, I felt I needed a way to help you "meet" them and keep them straight. They are alike and yet different in so many ways. Before they took time off, many had interesting careers, loving families, and what seemed like the picture of success. The one fallout? They were starved for time for themselves.

I thank them for being so open about their experiences and lessons learned. Our shared agenda is to help other good girls see the light and take a little time off for good behavior.

This is a snapshot of the women in this book, "Before Time Off," in order of appearance:

Eileen, fifty-two, married, mother of a thirteen-year-old, living in New Canaan, Connecticut, had just been laid off as a magazine publishing executive after a successful career.

Lisa K., married and living in Connecticut with two young children, is a marketing executive in a large consumer products company when she confronts breast cancer at thirty.

Peggy, fifty-three, married, heads a nonprofit advertising organization in New York and turned down an offer of paid time off when she was single and thirty-eight.

Monique, forty, married with a nine-year-old daughter, editor in chief of *Essence* magazine, from Brooklyn, New York, struggles to write a book called *Having What Matters* when she's not "having what matters" in her own life.

Donna D., married with an eleven-year-old son, is a human resources executive for Procter & Gamble in Cincinnati, Ohio, when she was offered a voluntary retirement package at forty-one.

Lisa B., thirty-five, a single superstar working overtime in the online travel business, had put her personal life on hold in Dallas, Texas.

Courtney, thirty-two, single, a Silicon Alley entrepreneur, publisher, and party host before the dot-com bubble burst, was called "the Contessa of Tribeca."

Ann, forty-seven, married, three daughters aged eighteen, twenty-one, and twenty-three, business publication editor, living in Bronxville, New York, plans for time off until reality sets in.

Rosemary, forty, single, founder and head of a corporate child-care company in Boston, sees a management changeover as an opportunity for changing her life.

Camille, forty-two, married with two children, eight and eleven, president of a New York literary public relations firm, dreams of a year with her family in Rome.

Kerry, thirty, married, a fast climber in public relations, sees the World Trade Center collapse and questions her future.

Donata, forty-one, of Marin County, California, an entertaining expert with Williams Sonoma, married with an eighteen-year-old stepson and three-year-old son, awakens to a new opportunity while on a beach vacation.

Bonnie, fifty, married and a senior executive who helped lead the turnaround at Houston's Continental Airlines is offered a retirement package at fifty.

Lalita, forty-six, single, a high-ranking executive in Sun Microsystems, Silicon Valley, California, elects for a huge life change.

Debra, forty-six, married with an eight-year-old son and four-year-old twin boy and girl, senior executive of a consumer products company, from Westchester, New York, is not working for the first time in twenty-five years.

Isa, thirty-three, single, senior customer service executive in a Silicon Valley technology company, races between hectic high-tech days and her nights as a dancer and artist.

Ardith, forty, a senior marketing executive with Clairol, living in New York City and commuting to Connecticut, is faced with a choice, thanks to a company merger.

Joan, forty-seven, married, mother of a thirteen-year-old daughter, daydreams about quitting her intense job as an executive vice president in specialty retail in Columbus, Ohio.

Diana, forty-eight, married, with a twenty-one-year-old daughter in college and a son entering high school, owner of a communications business in Boston, questions when she'll ever be ready for time off.

Julie, thirty-four, single, is a principal in a Washington, D.C. –based consulting firm with a yen to travel.

Peri, thirty-three, married, executive at New York City ad agency Lowe & Partners, confronts a crisis when her first daughter is born.

Liz, forty and single, leaves a marquee marketing job in Portland, Oregon, to create a life that's as creative as it is meaningful.

Pam, thirty-seven, is a single New Yorker who's successful, if disillusioned, as an executive at a direct marketing agency.

Kay, forty-two, married, decides to leave her job as a trial lawyer at a downtown New York City law firm to spend time with her two small children—on the Friday before September 11, 2001.

Diane, fifty-one, single in New York, already with a stellar career, survives a near-death car accident and remakes her life.

Donna G., forty-four, a single New Yorker, responsible for consumer products at World Wrestling Entertainment, is reluctant to take her vacation, let alone a break.

Karen J., married, executive producer at a New York creative services company, finally has the baby she's wanted at thirty-eight.

Leslie, twenty-six, a married human resources manager in a division of Allied Chemical in New York City, faces the fear of a very sick baby son.

Jane C., forty-one, married with three stepsons and a little daughter ready to start preschool, plans a sabbatical from her job teaching high school in Pennsylvania.

Cindy, thirty-three, single, director of a consulting firm in New York City, was faced with a decision: make a critical work deadline or eulogize a best friend.

Jane B., fifty-two, who was single, headed human resources for a global company in New York, battles personal and professional hardships before surrendering to a break.

Marsha, fifty-two, married with two adult sons, living in Montclair, New Jersey, successfully navigated multiple careers while raising children, but faces an unfinished piece of personal business.

Marilyn leaves a successful career in real estate law at fifty and looks to her avocation in design as a second life phase.

Catherine, fifty-one, married, one child, New York retail fashion marketer, changes from career to career in seven-year cycles.

Karen N., of San Rafael, California, is married with an eighteen-year-old daughter when she has a newborn son at forty, and leaves a high-level post in design and manufacturing to stay home with him.

Terry, forty-two, is a single executive in the investment industry in San Francisco, California, who's overworked and underappreciated.

Barbara, forty, married and the mother of three small children, is a literary public relations executive in Austin, Texas, looking for more time with her kids.

And Mary Lou, forty-five, married CEO of New York ad agency NW Ayer and Partners, is burning the candle at both ends and craving a break.

CHAPTER ONE

My Story

"Sister, Sister, call on me!" I can still hear my high-pitched first grade voice, shouting those first Type A good girl words to Sister Thomas Anice. It was the fall of 1959 in St. Helena's School in Philadelphia and I was already in a hurry to succeed.

In my navy blue uniform, I looked just like the other sixty-five kids in the class, but my attitude set me apart. I was the kind of kid you wish you could decaffeinate. I talked fast, a bundle of energy hellbent on getting As from the start. I was the first-born child of Mary and Ray Finlayson, who had waited several years for me. For the next forty years, I never let up.

Recently I looked through my dad's beat-up aluminum suitcase, which holds our family mementos, where I found some clues to my Type A roots. Digging among his love letters to Mom, faded family snapshots, and my worn tap shoes, I found my grammar school report cards. Ironically, each one was well preserved in its own brown envelope sponsored by Theodore Geitner, our neighborhood funeral director, which I thought was a little morbid. Inside, the story of my childhood was written in perfect Palmer Method As, not only for arithmetic and history, but for "behavior subjects," like Perseverance, Obedience, Self-control, Cleanliness, and Cooperation. My dad's proud "John R. Finlayson" approved every A, year after year.

One truly prophetic grade got my attention: A for perfect attendance, nearly every year from first to eighth grade. How did I go all those years, with barely a bellyache to keep me home? I remember insisting to my mom, "I feel good enough to go in, I can't miss today!" Once I had hung the first of those Perfect Attendance certificates on my bedroom wall, I refused to break my record. I was Mary Louise Finlayson, the good girl who was afraid not to show up and be called on.

I was a relentlessly cheerful child, eager to please my parents and teachers. Nicknames like Smiley and Bright Eyes fit me, though Goody Two Shoes might have been whispered out of earshot. In my dance recital pictures, I was the one with eyes straight to camera, tapskirt pulled out to the limits, and a face that said, "Please like me!"

Type A from the Start

I was a latchkey kid before it was fashionable, so in the free afterschool hours, I volunteered to stay late to straighten the desks and clap the chalk off the erasers. I never turned down a chance for extra credit work. I treasured the rewards of my good behavior, like JFK silver dollars and Pope John XXIII holy cards from the nuns.

In eighth grade, I received the greatest honor of all. It wasn't just being named one of four students out of a class of 225 to win the General Excellence Award. It was recognition of a higher order. Along with a handful of other girls, I was chosen to go down to the basement of the convent to wash the nuns' laundry at lunchtime. It was an honest to God thrill. It meant that on the most personal level, the "women in charge" trusted me. I had risen above my lowly schoolgirl status. (Plus, since all their stuff was labeled, I got to see who wore which size underwear.)

I was a self-reliant girl who shunned team sports and chorale groups. I liked going solo as the number one jump roper at recess, the lead dancer in school shows, or the class spelling bee champ. Competing that way was riskier, but I preferred counting on myself, and I admit, getting all the glory. I was in a hurry to win and no one could stop me.

Mom and Dad's Good Girl

I got my hunger for hard work from a mother who had a "real job" when most mothers stayed home. By night, she cooked our dinners, cleaned the house, and wrapped the next day's Velveeta sandwiches in wax paper. But by day, Mom worked in advertising. She loved working, and talked about her job every night at dinner. Yet she was also a chronic quitter. She took her red-haired temperament to the office and if by her morning coffee break she didn't like the agency anymore, she would call Dad, and say, "Ray, take me home. I hate this place." She knew she'd find something better the next day.

My mom often gave me permission to drop out, saying, "If you don't want to go to that rehearsal, it's okay." But I never took her up on it.

Unlike my career-loving mom, my dad taught me a different lesson about work. Dad was the service manager for an office machine company. He never seemed to really enjoy his job of satisfying irritated customers. He harbored dreams of being an architect or designer, and redesigned our row house every few years for the fun of it. His work never followed him home. Dad's true passion was our family.

In his quiet way, my dad was the one who set the expectations for my younger brother, Jack, and me. We grew up in a pay-for-performance household. Dad rewarded us with one dollar for first honors, eighty-five cents for second. I guess we'd have earned seventy-five cents for third, but we were so terrified of disappointing him and ourselves with Cs that we never dared to find out.

To this day, the words that I fear most from my dad are, "I'm disappointed in you." (Later in my career, I would dread the same from every boss.)

My parents' mantra was, "You can do and be anything you want to be," and I believed them. They'd always add the corollary: "But we will love you no matter what you decide to do." I only listened to the first part of their promise. I wanted to live up to their belief in me. I set out to prove that I could do pretty much anything I set my mind to.

Looking back, I realize how much their confidence made me believe that if I did the right thing, I would succeed. I got an early lesson in the flaw in that logic. I lost a citywide spelling bee on the word "dependant." (I spelled it with an "e-n-t," which is also correct, but we didn't contest the judges' call until too late.) Standing before their desk, I started to tear up over the unfairness of it all. To end the awkward incident, my dad told the judges, "We concede." (I had to ask him what that meant and how to spell it.) Injustice has always been hard for me to accept. Accepting failure has been even harder.

Teenage Type A

The little kid As transformed into high school ones. I kept raising the bar for what was "good." I got into advanced placement classes. I followed the rules (except for the time I got detention for hiking up my skirt after school). I didn't put peroxide in my hair or a cigarette between my lips. The years passed with straightened teeth and more straight As.

I entered LaSalle College in 1971, just as the women's movement was heating up. The school had gone coed the year before, and the ratio of men to women was four to one. It was great for my social life and even better training for a corporate career. But the lessons cut both ways. One day, the guys lined up outside the student center. They held a pile of placards, each marked with a number, one through ten. As women walked into the cafeteria, they graded us on looks. I was too embarrassed to look, but still A-obsessed enough to want the ten.

During college, I put my greatest energy into theater. I was chosen for the lead role in the school's performance of a retro musical comedy, *Dames at Sea*, the story of a stage neophyte who takes over when the faux show's diva gets sick. As Ruby, I gamely tap-danced my way out of the chorus line. It was a preview of what I hoped my career might be.

Between honors classes, my part-time bank teller job, and my rehearsal schedule, I was already riding the work/life balance roller coaster, but to me, it was normal. Halfway through college, I transferred to Saint Joseph's College, run by the Jesuits in Philadelphia. Those were really happy years. Good grades, good friends, and still good behavior. I was an anachronism in the seventies, as neither a rebel nor a bra burner. I was a good girl with a Farah Fawcett haircut, set on dean's list or bust.

Good Goes to Work

When I graduated from Saint Joe's, I planned to follow Mom into advertising. I identified sixteen agencies in downtown Philadelphia and put on a turquoise polyester minidress that I had sewn myself. I teetered into interviews on platform sandals with my résumé, proudly proclaiming not only my dramatic roles but my hair and eye color, my height and my weight. Unfortunately, the outfit and the stats got me nowhere on Philly's Madison Avenue.

I slumped back to my bank teller station and widened my net. That year, the job pickings were slim. I interviewed to be a travel agent, a vending machine inspector, and a textbook editor. I met with Union Carbide on a construction site. "See this map, sweetie," the fellow said, "you could sell car batteries to garages from here (he indicated Boston) all the way to here (Maryland.)" How fast did my platforms blow out of there?

I even auditioned to be the cohost of a college bowl game show hosted by Scott Tissue Paper. Being an on-air toilet bowl spokesperson never struck me as odd. I think I lost out to a weather girl.

My college came to the rescue with an offer from my advertising professor, Dan DeLucca, who had just been promoted to head of college relations and development. He offered me the huge sum of $9,500 a year to write fund-raising proposals. It wasn't advertising, but it was a writing job. That "yes" would begin the next twenty-three years of never saying "no" to work.

Happily Over My Head

My success strategy from the start was to be over my head as often as possible. For example, in 1976, the college commemorated its 125th anniversary. At twenty-two, I coordinated the entire event for six thousand people, including dignitaries like the head of the Jesuits in Rome and the late Princess Grace of Monaco.

For six months, I worked around the clock to make the celebration perfect. I got my first taste of being exhausted and overwhelmed by work. But I shook it off. Despite losing too much weight from running myself ragged, I was already addicted to the charge of making success happen.

As a reward, I was promoted to head of public relations, writing all college press releases and publications. I was the youngest person on the college administration, and one of the few women.

While working in the PR job, I met Joe Quinlan, who would become my husband. First, he was a friend and a career counselor. Where I was high voltage, Joe was calm and easy-going. A news reporter, he coached me on how to deal with the Philadelphia media. Even more valuable, he advised me on how to deal with men, how they thought and how to solve problems with them. As months went by, networking over lunch turned to love. He asked me to marry him on a fence in a South Jersey R/V campground where my parents had parked their Airstream. Romantic? I felt like I was in the movies.

Then Joe did the unthinkable for someone from Philadelphia. He got a job in New York City. He was hired as a TV news reporter for a new nightly news show called *The MacNeil/Lehrer Report*. I knew I had to get my own big-city job.

If You Can Make It Here

I tried to get an advertising job, but my nonprofit credentials didn't fly in New York. So I followed up on a friend's connection to Avon. I took the elevator to their headquarters, and the doors parted to reveal a panoramic view of Central Park. Beautifully dressed women were handing out lipsticks for a promotion. Our Lady of Cosmetics! I had arrived.

Avon didn't think I was qualified to be in public relations or advertising, but they thought I was enthusiastic and a good listener. They offered me a job as a recruiter in human resources, which was then called personnel, to hire assistants, who were then called secretaries. But my goal from day one was to be in their advertising department.

I approached my new job as if I were signing on for life. I figured, as long as they're paying me, I'm theirs. I wore only Avon makeup for the next ten years. I recently found an old jewelry box where every piece inside was made by Avon.

From the beginning, I had a mental picture of success as a ladder to the sky. I never envisioned a glass ceiling. But what haunted me was that it just kept going up with no end in sight. No relief or detour, just more steps.

After a few months, the job of company newsletter editor opened up. I took home a couple of old issues, redesigned the four-page monthly to a biweekly eight pager (it was the precomputer late seventies, so I cut and pasted it by hand), with new features, columns, and executive interviews. I got the job. The lessons stuck. Focus on what you want. Do something above and beyond to prove you can do it. Reach for the next rung of the ladder. Working overtime helps you get ahead. Good girl lessons for success.

Raising the Stakes

I was constantly setting aggressive goals. I planned to be a manager in two years and a director in five. In both cases, I made it and was one of the youngest at my level. By ten years, I expected to be a vice president. I figured that if I lasted till my fifties, I could hope to be president of Avon. I was a lifer.

At Avon, the highest accolade for a rising executive was, "she's got a strong sense of urgency," which meant persistence in the face of obstacles. I got into the habit of setting tighter deadlines than necessary and beating them. I had that sense of urgency, another Type A trademark in spades.

I continued to reach farther over my head. I was promoted to sales incentive manager to run a trip to Hawaii. I had never been to Hawaii or planned a vacation other than spring break, but I was responsible for taking one thousand Avon representatives to Honolulu.

We hired Bert Parks, who had just been fired as the longtime emcee of the Miss America pageant, to host a live award show to be teleconferenced from Hawaii, with medals, mink coats, and me as his onstage cohost. (I admit there were visions of "Ruby redux" in my head.) We pulled it off, which led to another promotion. And another.

In 1986, my Avon mentor, Diane Perlmutter, promoted me to director of advertising, my dream job. My learning curve skyrocketed as I handled multimillion-dollar budgets. I thrived on the pace and creativity.

But after ten years, I started to fall out of love with Avon. The company had gone through tremendous turmoil in the late eighties. I privately railed against new policies that weren't the "Avon way." It was no longer the place where I had grown up. I began to enjoy working with the folks at our ad agency more than my Avon colleagues.

Sensing my waning enthusiasm, Diane asked me, "When was the last time you felt happy to wake up and go to work?" My good girl reflex was to answer, "A few weeks ago." Then I looked in her doubting eyes and confessed, "Two, three, maybe six months." She knew. My sense of urgency had evolved to a maniacal sense of "do more and do it now." I was so consumed by work that I flicked on the hallway lights each morning, and worked till the nighttime cleaning crew arrived. Leaving Avon, even considering it, seemed like a betrayal. I had never even put together a résumé. I just kept thinking, If I stick it out, things will get better. Remember my A in Perseverance?

I didn't take action until I was passed over for a promotion. Another woman got my A. I scheduled an interview for an ad agency job. Fifteen minutes into the interview, they offered me a position as vice president, account director. I thought it was because I was smart. Now I know it was because they were assigning me to their toughest client and they saw I had the dogged attitude to take them on.

I resigned from Avon and sobbed as I packed away each memory. I even took my framed Principles That Guide Avon plaque. Rather than toss it, I gently placed a personal photograph over the corporate calligraphy. It's still in my office to this day. I wasn't leaving a job. I was leaving home.

On My Best Behavior

Wanted: Ad agency person who will do anything and everything because she doesn't know any better.

My first job foretold the rest. My role was to keep the agency from getting fired. I believed I could convert unhappy clients into wonderful partners. But angry clients devour agencies and my can-do attitude made me the perfect snack.

In advertising, many people sign on at twenty-one and burn out or leave before forty. I started at thirty-five, naïve but passionate. Being green was an advantage. I was willing to hang coats when my peers, nearly all male, were settling behind the big desk, awaiting the next client golf game. I moved up fast in my next ten years, several times being named as the youngest, the first, the only woman at my level.

I fell in love with the pace and the informal atmosphere of advertising—it was just what my mom had talked about at the dinner table years before and what I had grown up wanting. But I understimated how the intensity of a service environment would consume so much more of my life. In advertising, there's normal time and there's client time. I started to live my days on "client time," which means you're always there, always on, always ready for more, and always smiling. (I still believe that Catholic school was the best training for advertising account management.) Being in client service was central casting for a Type A good girl.

Time Off Gone By

When Joe and I were first married, we took vacations. I remember trips in the eighties that lasted two weeks. When I was gone, I was *gone*.

But during the nineties, the stakes went up. My salary increased, my duties matched the pay, and I was responsible for things that were largely out of my control... creative people, successful ads, and demanding clients. After two years at my first agency, I was recruited to another, again for a client that was threatening to leave. I was given the additional role of head of new business. Pitching and winning millions of dollars of business was alluring for a score-obsessed woman like me. I took the challenge, thinking, I can work harder. I did, and vacations started to disappear.

We settled for the occasional long weekend instead. Eventually, my perspective deteriorated to the point where I'd refer to an industry convention as "going on vacation."

The quality of the time off changed, too. Technology was partly to blame. Voicemail became a lifeline. I'd stop frequently at pay phones, "just to get it off my mind." Sometimes I sneaked calls when

I was supposed to be relaxing. I felt I had to be connected or at least contribute my two cents to supposedly save the day.

Back home, evenings became my second shift. Our sofa became a surrogate office, with mail and documents ripe for reading after dinner. I used to test myself to see how fast I could answer clients' requests. I became impatient with people who weren't as "urgent" as I was. I forgot that everyone isn't Type A. That weeknights and weekends were supposed to be for resting, not working.

My days were packed with everyone else's agendas. I always thought the "open door" policy was a sign of a great manager. Unfortunately, everyone's favorite open door time seemed to come at around 5:30 or 6:00 P.M. "Do you have a few minutes?" My answer was nearly always yes. Sometimes I resented it, but I have to admit I often secretly enjoyed it. These people were my family and if they needed me, my job was to be there for them. I could always get home a little later.

The Good Girl No One Knew

Other women often ask me whether I have kids. When I say no, I get a look that hints, "Oh, then you didn't have it as bad as I did." Since I've interviewed thousands of moms about their lives, I'm the first to say that moms have the toughest jobs of all. If stress is a contest, they win.

But stress isn't a contest. Not having kids made me work even longer hours. I didn't have children begging me to come home, or causing me to turn down business trips. Though it's anything but time off, I never had those weeks or months of maternity leave. Without the pull of children, I could take on more and drive harder.

Not having kids wasn't a choice. Until my husband and I were both thirty-five, we just weren't ready. But as time ticked by, we decided to go for it. We couldn't have known that we were in for years of fertility treatments, a marathon of needles and drugs and tests. I would rush to the doctor's office early in the morning or at lunchtime. I'd walk right back into a meeting without a pause or a comment. I never told anyone at work about this. I didn't want it to seem like I wasn't 100 percent dedicated, which might eliminate me from a possible promotion. I even downplayed it to my parents, so I wouldn't worry them.

No matter how much I followed the doctor's rules, I couldn't get an A. Sitting in the waiting room each month, I couldn't accept that I was failing at something so basic. I was angry, frustrated, and tired. After four years, and eventually surgery, I gave up. No answer. No baby. By then, we were so wrung out and disappointed, we just decided to count our blessings and move on. Anyway, there was more work to do.

Crossing the Line

In the late eighties, we bought a small weekend house in Pennsylvania. I promised that no "work work" would be done or spoken in that house, but that promise was soon forgotten. My phone bill showed sixty calls to my voicemail one weekend. Time "off" was still time "on." I thought my work was more important than relaxing. Though Joe would get frustrated with my growing workaholic style, he was supportive of my success, which only gave me the room to work harder.

Friendships also took a backseat to work. We would attend Broadway shows together and I'd bolt at intermission to go home to work. I was usually late and sometimes a no-show to friends' events. I like to believe that I am a good friend, but for those years, I know I wasn't. I depended on my friends and family to understand how important my job was, how much the money mattered, how "just one more assignment" would make a big difference and serve as an excuse to miss dates, be late, and cancel too many personal plans.

Instead, I started to connect more with my work friends. We had so much in common, every up and down, the latest gossip or road trip. But unlike lifelong friends, I couldn't really open up with them. My job was to keep them in the "everything's okay" zone, even when everything wasn't.

Too often, my employees, colleagues, clients, and bosses got the best of my love. Their phone calls were returned immediately. I never missed their meetings. I celebrated their birthdays with presents and parties. I let them cry on my shoulder. I can't say the same for the way I treated the people I really loved, or the way I treated myself. I gave myself little empathy or downtime. When I received résumés that listed applicants' hobbies, I felt annoyed and jealous. I'd wonder, What's my hobby? Meetings?

CEO or Bust

At the age of thirty-nine, I was asked to be president of the New York office of NW Ayer, the oldest advertising agency in the United States. As someone who measured progress by age milestones, making president before forty was a big deal. But, even with responsibility for five hundred staffers and nearly a half billion dollars in billings with major national clients, I didn't feel I had arrived. I had so much more to prove.

Instead of being hired to save a client, I was hired to save an agency. I felt responsible for turning around a business that had suffered tremendous losses. I thought I could do it by working harder, applying the full force of my creativity and being a tireless advocate for the clients, the people, and the agency's image. I felt even more beholden to "the cause."

The early months were exhilarating. We won the multimillion-dollar Avon account. I hired some new talent. We were invited to high-profile new business pitches. However, while trying to overcome our past, internal tensions erupted and the chairman and CEO who hired me suddenly left. And I was the CEO apparent. "Left holding the bag" might have been a better description, which indeed became clear when the calls from the major news media started pouring in: Why did he leave? What are you going to do? How do the clients feel?

Those were fair questions, since to huge, conservative clients like ours—Procter & Gamble, General Motors, AT&T, and Avon—a steady agency was critical. Most of the clients were supportive, but DeBeers, the diamond company, was not so sanguine.

Fifty-seven years before, a female Ayer copywriter had written the famous line, "A diamond is forever." With one devastating phone call, I learned that it wasn't. I pushed on.

I was one of only a handful of female CEOs of a national agency in 1995. Stepping into that role brightened the spotlight on me. I had a beautiful corner office, a view of the Statue of Liberty, even my own bathroom. Well-situated, but in over my head, I was an example of "beware of what you wish for." The buck stopped with me. I had mounting responsibilities and a killer calendar to match.

The Addictive Agenda

When I picture my old desk calendar, I see a lot of ink. The days were chopped into half-hour chunks, starting with a breakfast meeting, lunch with a client, late hours, capped off with evening work events. There were very few blank spaces, and when I found one, I'd fill it with someone's need. But the hardest hours didn't appear on the day planner.

The Mary Lou who set out each morning was energetic, dressed to the nines, with a big, perky smile. But most nights, a different woman returned to the apartment. I'd drag in late, pale and tired, looking for a glass of chardonnay and a takeout menu. Joe and I would eat the delivery du jour, and I'd talk about work. By 10:00 P.M., I'd fall into bed, and within seconds of hitting the pillow, I'd be out. But at 2:00 A.M., my eyes would flash to stare at the digital clock and the office would invade the bedroom. I'd learn much later that this fitful sleep was a warning sign of severe stress and anxiety.

I'd tiptoe to the living room and listen to voicemails and make lists. I left messages, thinking my employees would see how committed I was. Looking back, I imagine "committed" was what they wanted to have done to me.

I'd pace and worry till 4:00 A.M., then pass out until the alarm buzzed me bolt awake at 6:30 A.M. to do it all over again.

I was worn out. I had always been one of those women who looked young for her age, and people would say, "No way you're forty!" As the pressure mounted and the sleep eluded me, those compliments vaporized. Lack of exercise put me out of condition. No amount of undereye concealer could hide the dark circles. Sometimes my image in the mirror stopped me in my tracks. Who was that tired woman?

The Wrong Call

My fixation on getting an A as CEO got me an F as a daughter one weekend in 1997.

On a Saturday morning, my mom called from Florida. Her usually upbeat voice was almost inaudible. "I'm in the hospital," she whispered.

"What's wrong with you?" I asked.

"It's your dad . . . he's had a stroke."

Within two hours, I was on a flight to Fort Myers, praying my dad would be all right. My brother and I were so scared. Dad improved and passed some critical timelines, and kept saying, "You kids should go back to work." I said I would stay, but I knew I was supposed to be on a long-planned trip to see our largest client.

I was wavering on whether to cancel. But with my dad's urging, the Type A good girl got on a plane. I decided I could wake up at dawn the next day, fly for five hours, attend the meeting, and get back to Florida by midnight.

The meeting started late and the conversation was inconsequential. Late that night, I dragged back to my mom and dad's house.

Why had I gone? What was wrong with me that I couldn't say no? What if something had happened to Dad while I was in a meeting? My dad got better every day. I promised to straighten out my priorities. But I don't remember changing at all.

Getting What You Wish For

I should have known things were bad when I started to fantasize about devious ways to get time off. I was performing too well to get fired. And if I got fired, I wouldn't get severance. How could I escape? Perhaps a small accident? I figured if I stepped off a curb and broke my ankle or a car hit me—not hard enough to kill me, just enough to put me in the hospital—then I would get some time off.

In a sick way, I got my wish and it still didn't work. One morning, I did my usual halfhearted workout. Then I hailed a cab to the office where I was scheduled to make a presentation to a toilet paper manufacturing client.

Suddenly, the cab made a lefthand turn into the path of an oncoming car. A black sedan barreled into the rear passenger door. I heard the crunch, then silence.

I froze, doing a mental body scan, and I whispered to the driver, "Help me, something hurts in my back." He turned to look at me and laughed. He got out of the cab and walked away.

My first thought was to escape, but the door was smashed shut. Wincing, I slid gingerly across the backseat, and pulled myself out of the cab to wave down another.

On my way home, every bump was agony. Our apartment building's security guard rushed out to the cab and called 911 and buzzed Joe, who was upstairs. By the time my husband came out to the sidewalk, the EMS guys were strapping me to a board to lift me into an ambulance. I was terrified. An X-ray turned up two broken ribs, which, compared to my fears, wasn't bad, but I couldn't breathe without aching.

The accident should have been scary. But the really scary part was when I asked Joe if he had called my office. I was still worried about the client presentation. "Oh yeah," Joe said casually, "Melissa told the client you couldn't make it."

Still bound to a gurney, I went ballistic. "WHAT DO YOU MEAN, SHE SAID I COULDN'T 'MAKE' IT? GIVE ME YOUR CELL PHONE!" I shouted at my assistant, "Tell the client that I would NEVER just 'miss' a meeting! I was in an accident and I'll be back tomorrow."

That really spooked Joe. Years later he confessed that he wondered, Who is this woman who was almost killed and panicked about missing a stupid toilet paper meeting? I don't remember thinking it was strange at all. My mind went straight to worrying that the client was thinking I hadn't shown up, that I hadn't cared.

I was back at work within a day.

Out of Time

Over the course of my last couple of years as CEO, I went through some pretty tough business circumstances. Two longtime clients called it quits. Our owner privately put the agency up for sale. The stress of not knowing where this multimillion-dollar business was headed while keeping a cheerfully stiff upper lip was a daily strain. While the ownership issues roiled, I hit the road to reassure our clients.

Soon, the travel miles were out of control. I joked that I was like a human FedEx package. Once I was so determined not to miss a flight that I yanked off my high heels and ran barefoot from one end of an airport to the other.

The public pressure and attention increased. I used to feel that the trade press caught so many of our tiniest missteps that I expected one day to read in the papers when I'd had a bad hair day. I felt like the poster child for agency unrest. To help our image, I decided to be even more aggressively "on," visible and positive. I'd attend two or three black tie industry events in a week. Once, I hit three in the same night. I could change from a business suit to an evening dress in an airplane bathroom. I could do my hair and makeup in the back of a speeding cab. All in the line of duty.

Thankfully, NW Ayer was bought by a global network, the MacManus Group, which was prepared to invest in our rebirth. The chairman of the group, Roy Bostock, an advertising veteran, had deep and long relationships with our biggest clients. It was the first time in years I had a calm and knowing hand above me. I felt excited to begin to rebuild the agency under his guidance.

We won major global accounts like Continental Airlines, and the workload kicked up. Things were turning around. I won some prestigious awards. I was named Advertising Woman of the Year by the Advertising Women of New York and received the Matrix Award from New York Women in Communications. The honors only made me turn up the heat. There was nothing I wouldn't do to justify anyone's faith in me, especially my family's.

The attention, which I know I enjoyed, also increased my fear of failing and my daily anxiety. My mom and dad, though proud of my success, would confide that they were worried that I was doing too much. "Take it easy, come stay with us for a while," they'd say. But I ignored their advice. I thought they were just being loving parents. Joe would say, "You don't need this. Why don't you leave?" I felt he was just being too soft on me. I could take it.

My sense of humor was gone. I had become edgy and short-tempered. Once I was so angry at a colleague, I punctuated my tirade with a slammed door that almost shattered glass. The smiling "Mary Sunshine" was turning into someone I didn't like very much.

Throughout my career, my hallmark had been my enthusiastic attitude. But if I had to personify myself during those last exhausting months, it would be as the character Sigourney Weaver plays in the movie *Ghostbusters* when she morphs into Zuul, the snarling monster on the roof. I was impatient and humorless and unsympathetic. "He's out sick again?" shrieked Miss Perfect Attendance.

"She's taking another day off?" said the woman who desperately needed one herself. Mine was no longer the voice of a leader, nor a good girl.

I remember a particular Monday morning when I got into the elevator with a coworker. And as we rode up, she said, "You know, each day I think how glad I am that you are running this agency, because this job is the only support for me and my daughter." I felt crushingly bad when she said that, because all I could think was, If she only knew how much financial pressure we are under and how worried I am that her job might not be secure. She must have sensed it, because she added, "But I guess that's a lot of weight right here, right?" and she touched her shoulders. My eyes filled with tears at the truth of what she'd said. But I just smiled.

Hating to Lose

By 1998, the marketplace was extremely tough for midsize agencies like ours. Meganetworks could beat us with resources and clout. Tiny boutiques could outcreate us without the scrutiny of big-name clients. We were losing ground. But my job was to keep the morale up. Every time I let my worry show, rumors flew.

I had to cut staff as a way to find the dollars to make up for the losses. Given my personal relationships with so many of the people, every one of those firings ate at me. There were times that I envied the people I let go. Many had good exit packages. Some walked out with a new attitude about their lives. A part of me wished I could follow them.

In my last year as CEO, I hit an emotional turning point, following a pitch for an insurance company that we admired. The contest was extended to an extra shoot-out round between ourselves and another contender.

We needed the business so badly and worked so hard to land it. That's why, when a few days later, the client called to say we had lost, I couldn't even speak. Hurt and angry tears rolled down my face as I closed my office door, dreading having to break the bad news. (Seven years later, I ran into that insurance client. He still remembered how difficult it was for him to make that call. It felt good to tell him that thanks to his "no," I finally made a change in my life. It was a blessing in disguise.)

A Reprieve

In September of 1998, a concerned friend of mine asked me if I'd ever thought of taking a leave. She said, "If you lived in Europe and you were this worn-out, you'd get a prescription for some time away." Was I that bad? Could I really take some extended time off? In all those years of working, I had never even considered the idea. I never knew anyone who had done that, especially while they were still in a high-stakes job. But as soon as she said it, I knew that I would. That I had to. Or else.

It was as if she had dumped a bucket of ice water on me to wake me up out of my stressed-out dream world. Once awake, I was determined to stay that way. I decided to make a move fast before I chickened out. I didn't want anyone to talk me out of it.

In hindsight, I realize I should have been worried about the consequences of asking for time off. What if I lost my big job and everything that went with it? Worse, what if I fell off everyone's Rolodex? Who would I be if I were no longer a corporate person? I just kept asking myself, What is the worst thing that could happen if I ask? And all I could come up with was, My boss will say no and I will have to keep going. But I knew I couldn't keep going for one more day. So my choice was to ask for some time and trust he'd say yes . . . or be prepared to quit. I had nothing to lose, really, but my exhaustion.

My first mission was to tell Joe. Over dinner, I told him that I wanted to stop working for a while. I finally understood what he had seen all along. Outside on the sidewalk, we held each other tightly. It was time to stop running. He wanted me back the way he knew me. His joy was the first sign I'd made the right decision.

That weekend, I told my parents and my brother. I was concerned that they'd think I was risking all I'd worked for. "Thank God," my mom said, "we've been so worried about you." They knew how long and how hard I had been going at it. Jack agreed. I had permission to bail from the people I wanted to please so much.

I shouldn't have been surprised. There was a moment not long before, when I was getting ready to go onstage to accept my Advertising Woman of the Year Award. My dad came over to me. "I'm so proud of you," he said, "but I'd be just as proud if you were wiping down counters in a diner." It was just what he had said to me so long ago: "You can be anything you want, but we will love you no matter what you decide." Why did it take me so long to listen?

I prepared to talk to my boss, Roy Bostock, who had been an incredible supporter. More than anyone, he knew what I had been through as CEO of a volatile business. I focused on agency issues until I got to the last page of "to-dos" for the following year. I said, "I know that all these things need to be done, but right now, I'm not the one to do it. I'm exhausted, and I need some time off." I asked for five weeks. (I decided that was a palatable middle ground between the month I was owed and the six weeks that might seem sort of Betty Ford–ish.)

Roy looked at me, and his face softened. I believe he was reflecting on his own thirty-five-year career of sticking it out. He said yes. I was shocked.

In a final show of my good girl DNA, I showed him a list of nine prescheduled client events that I intended to attend during my five weeks out. "Give me a pen," he said. And he drew a line through the page. "Make this the most selfish time of your life. If you come back for these events, you'll ruin what you're setting out to do." Selfish. That's not even in the good girl dictionary.

Starting to Stop

The next night I met with the women who respectively headed the account, new business, and PR areas of the agency. I asked if they would run the company for the next five weeks. "No calls, no messages, no mail," I said. "I don't want to know anything about the agency or the ad business. Whatever decisions you make, I agree with them already."

My plan was falling into place. With just a week to go (purposely short notice since I didn't want anyone talking me out of it or piling more work on my desk), I realized I had some basic housekeeping to do.

It sounds silly, but I didn't have any casual clothes, since my life was lived in high heels and suits. I bought some comfortable shoes and sweaters that I could wear during what I hoped would be daily jaunts in the cold fall sunshine.

A week before, I had bought a suit. It was black, of course, and very businesslike. When it arrived home, my mother, who was visiting, opened the box. After voicing her usual disgust with the price tag (and noting that I'd gone up a size), she said, "Are you sure you want this suit? After you've been out a while, you might not be the same person who'd wear this . . . you might even be a smaller size."

I took it back to the same woman I'd bought it from. "I'm returning this suit because I'm changing my life." Her eyes widened as she took it back. "Good luck," she whispered.

I bought a journal and a calendar, beautifully blank. I picked up a disposable camera and a scrapbook to keep track of the upcoming weeks. I signed on for just three things. I booked three days in a spa to jump-start my new good behavior. I registered for Latin dancing lessons on the four Monday nights. And I made plans to be in Florida for Thanksgiving with my parents and my brother, which would be a perfect ending to my time off.

I attended one last business conference before my leave. In a prophetic moment, a speaker described something called a "walkabout." He said it was an Aboriginal tradition where the leader of a tribe went out into the bush to think and gaze back at his life from afar in order to get perspective.

From that point on, I called my five weeks my walkabout. "Sabbatical" seemed formal and inflated for five weeks. And "vacation" didn't do it. I just wanted some perspective.

Walkabout

The first day I woke up without an alarm. It was October 22, 1998, my forty-fifth birthday. I truly had something to celebrate. I felt light, as if a huge weight had literally been lifted off my shoulders.

I got a cup of coffee and the newspaper and did the unthinkable. I sat in my living room with the sun streaming in and I sipped and read as long as I wanted. While this may sound pathetically normal, it was a first for me. We had moved into the apartment five years before, and when I left each morning, it was still dark. I sat there in the sunshine and asked myself, What do I want to do today? I asked myself that every day of the five weeks.

My happiest memories were the simplest ones, like eating breakfast in a neighborhood diner. One weekend out in the country, I attended an herbal wreath-making class in a barn. The last time I remembered sitting still for two hours, making a "craft," I was seven years old and making potholders. There I was, forty-five and sticking rosemary into straw and chatting over tea with strangers.

I didn't go from Type A to Type ZZZ. Not surprisingly, I turned out to be a Type A relaxer. By letting go of my lists to "do," I was filled with fresh energy to "be." I didn't do the TV-and-bonbons fantasy. I decided to decaffeinate myself and work out and go on a protein diet. I took Latin dancing lessons in a studio where you salsa with men you'll never see again. I went ice-skating in the middle of the afternoon for the fun of it. I took a kick-boxing class with my niece. I saw a movie by myself for the first time in years. I felt like a carefree kid. I felt like an independent woman. It was fun and physical and liberating.

Just walking around my own neighborhood in New York was a treat. I used to wonder about those people who sat in cafés or talked with friends on street corners. I assuaged my jealousy by assuming they were out-of-work dancers and actors. Now I was one of those café people. I loved the sheer blankness of the days, the empty space to fill, or not. I resisted the urge to do all the "when I get time" errands, like clean closets or organize photos. The "what do I really want to do today" question kept me busy enough.

I finally spent some real time with friends. My girlfriend Mary Lynn and I first met when we were high school freshmen. While I moved to New York, Mary Lynn stayed in Philadelphia and taught school. Her current love was teaching little kids to love poetry. All those years, yet I never knew what Mary Lynn's days were like. I drove to her school and sat in one of the tiny kid's desks and watched her teach.

I changed physically. I lost weight, increased my energy, became softer and easier. I looked different, even after just a week of being off. I was grinning all the time. My eyes were relaxed. I walked slower. I talked slower. I listened better. I even learned to enjoy shopping again. In the "old days," I'd hyperventilate and I'd shove my credit card across the counter, so I could get on with my "important" day. It's amazing what nice conversations you can have with perfect strangers when you're not manic.

My mind was finally free of the din of everyone else's needs and agendas, and in that quiet space, I could look inside myself and realize who I had turned out to be. I kept a journal for the first time in my life so I could record the changes and hear my own voice at last. Without the pressure to perform a role, even one I had once loved, I was able to think about the people in my life who mattered most. My priorities shifted back toward what was real, instead of what was required of me. The trappings of my overworked life, once removed, seemed unnecessary. Why did I feel I had to rush everywhere? How much higher on my unending ladder did I have to climb? Wasn't it time to figure out what I am really passionate about without the worry of pleasing everyone else?

At the spa I had an experience that would help me understand what I would do after the leave. There was a labyrinth on the property, made of stones assembled in an ever-tighter circular path from outside to the center. I was told that I should enter the labyrinth thinking of a question that's puzzling me. By walking slowly and turning that question over in my mind, I might come to a solution by the time I'd made it to the center and back. My question was, "What should I be doing with my career?" It was not something I expected a bunch of rocks to answer.

As the circle got smaller and smaller, I had a stunning realization. I had been defining my options for my career in smaller and smaller ways, all tightly wound around advertising. Would I go back to my job? Could I work at another agency? Should I go back to a client company? All were just variations on the same theme. When I got to the center of the circle, I thought, Why can't I do something outside of advertising? I'm good at other things. I like to write. I'm a good speaker. Why do I think I can only do ads?

I didn't try to figure it all out then. I went back to the business of doing nothing until my leave was nearly over. Then I took a blank piece of paper and drew a line down the center. At the top of the left side, I wrote, "What I love to do and am really good at." And at the top of the right, "What I hate to do and I am not very good at."

I filled in the "hate side" first. Quickly, it was evident that I had written the worst parts of my job description as CEO: handling difficult people, administrative tasks, managing things out of my control. On the "love side," I listed my passions. I loved to write, to speak, and to be onstage. I actually still enjoyed a lot of the client business, as long as it was coming up with ideas and not wrangling over whether ads were blue or red. I wanted to focus on women since I thought I could be an honest voice on their behalf, without the burden of selling ads. I even brazenly thought that I would get myself on TV. It was a list of my dreams, so why not?

Most of all, I knew I wanted to retain what I had gained during my weeks off—more easy time with my family and friends, more downtime to relax and think and create, more "up" time to exercise and be healthy, and as odd as it sounds for an overreaching Type A, more rest for the rest of my life.

At the end of the leave, celebrating Thanksgiving with my family, I rehearsed what I would say when I returned. Now I had a clear picture of what I wanted my life to be. And going back didn't mean going backward.

What It Felt Like to Go Back

When I walked into my office after five weeks away, I felt like I was in the second act of a play that I didn't belong in. Everyone looked strained. Everything needed to be done at crisis speed. As much as I wanted to talk about my time off, most people had limited interest. Several people seemed annoyed or jealous that I had been off while they held down the fort. Most of all, they seemed as if they were all still in the same bad meeting they'd been in the day I'd left.

I felt mellow and calm, almost as if I were in slow motion. A rumor circulated that I had had a facelift. I don't know what I looked like, but I do know that I didn't look as tired or old as before. I was relaxed and at the same time highly energized. And whether I was or not, I felt wise. The problems they told me about didn't seem so bad, given my new time-off perspective.

I knew in my bones I had to leave. I felt nervous as I walked into Roy's office. He had granted me my reprieve and expected my return. We made small talk, but I had to spill the truth. "I don't want to be CEO anymore. I have a new idea for a company. I wish I could still work with you, but I have to do this." I outlined the idea of a new business that was focused on listening to women. I would start to write and speak and create media out of what I learned.

Obviously, this wasn't what he was waiting to hear. But, in a stroke of remarkable good luck, he looked at it as a business opportunity. "I think it's an interesting concept. I'd like you to think about starting it here, as a division of the holding company." This was beyond my expectations.

Walking the Walk

Afterward, there were many days when I wondered, What have I done?

There were people who secretly believed that I had been fired or that I just couldn't take the heat of the job. When asked what I was up to, I described Just Ask a Woman. I didn't have any clients or products or anything. It was a little disconcerting at first, to be so loose, but day by day, I felt more convinced I could make a go of it.

My new business didn't become real until I spoke out loud about it. Each year, Cathie Black, president of Hearst Magazines, held a women-only getaway for her editors, publishers, and clients, called Mind, Body, Soul. I knew that I wanted to speak about changing my life, but I didn't know if it would resonate with the audience of high-charging, high-profile women.

I told my story of growing up and of how I had become CEO. I described what my job was like, reading verbatim from a typical week of my old calendar, which I brought onstage with me. "Monday started at eight with a breakfast meeting uptown, but then I had to get back for a nine with someone who wanted to quit. At nine-thirty, I had a client conference call about a creative problem. At ten, a financial meeting, and I knew that the numbers weren't good." And so on and so on . . . until Friday night. When I looked up, the room was pin-drop still because I was reading them the story of their own lives.

It was the first time I acknowledged publicly that I had walked away from a life that looked good on the outside, but hurt on the inside. There was no turning back after that.

To help make my new plan feel real, I devised a simple visual. I pictured a windowsill lined with flowerpots. Each pot held a different idea: consulting, books, media, speaking, training. I figured that I would "water" all of them, and see which one grew first or fastest. Consulting turned out to be the fast starter, which was not a surprise since it was closest to my past experience. And I knew that to become expert on women's needs, I'd need to listen . . . a lot.

Those first three years, I interviewed three thousand women. It was amazing to me how easily I adapted to the free-form nature of our tiny business after two decades in a corporate structure. I didn't miss advertising one single day.

I didn't give up on the other flowerpots. I started to write articles for women's magazines to stretch myself out of my years of memos. The third year, I got a contract to write a book about marketing to women. The fourth year, I traveled to promote the book, and ended up onstage as a speaker all over the country. Now, Just Ask a Woman is five years old.

Some former colleagues told me I had too many "flowerpots." Their world was all about "focus." My focus is doing what I love. And the flowerpots keep growing.

I admit I still have that Type A good girl DNA that obsesses over getting each assignment right, that wants every speech to be a showstopper. Despite our laid-back office and informal work style at Just Ask a Woman, and the support of the three wonderful women I work with, sometimes I still take on more than I should. The biggest difference is that now at least I've learned to draw lines. I say "no" to people and events that drag me down. And I say "yes" to those that give me joy and satisfaction. I'm busy doing what I love and I'm true to my passions.

My personal life is much richer because I protect my downtime and reserve it for myself and for family and friends, without the CEO clock ticking in my head. My days are more under my control since I don't "do" breakfast meetings and evenings are for Joe and me. We love to spend time with our dog Danny Boy, a furry symbol of my changed life. (Joe catches me when my "evil twin" occasionally pops up, and he helps me put her back where she belongs.) Time spent with my family is precious and inviolable. I read more, walk more, and breathe more. I smile a lot. I am deeply happy. And I sleep all the way through the night.

CHAPTER TWO

Growing Up Good

I am not the only Type A good girl. I've got a lot of company. Perhaps you're one yourself. Millions of us went to the same good girl training camp. Picture the women in your personal and professional circles, and you will easily identify the ones I mean. Think of your neighbor who says, "Leave it to me, I'll pick up all the kids." Imagine the colleague who cheerfully takes on the extra assignment or stays late to help you out. Phrases like, "No problem at all!" are tip-offs. Good girls are great to be around. We persevere and volunteer. We try to deliver 100 percent plus. We smile while doing it.

Ask any hardworking woman if she'd describe her growing-up self as a Type A good girl, and you'll get a knowing grin. Whether it's a matter of pride or regret, it's a badge many of us wear for life. As my friend Eileen put it, "From the day I hopped out of my crib, I was the Type A personality."

We grew up with Type A training wheels on the backs of our bikes. We paid attention to Mom and Dad. We did our homework. We got good grades. We sold the most Girl Scout cookies and practiced our instruments. We were impatient to succeed. And so we did.

We learned to speak the can-do code. "I try to give my best to everything I do." "If I say I'll do something, I do it." The good news about good girl roots is that they set us on a track of success and achievement. The bad news is that they can strangle us in an unending series of "shoulds" that keep us from letting go and having a life. The "gotta get an A" turns into a "gotta get that promotion." And good is never good enough.

The Anatomy of Type A

Type A behavior was first observed in the 1950s by two cardiologists who noticed that most of their heart attack patients shared certain traits, including "impatience, a sense of time urgency, an unrelenting urge for recognition and power, an unusual preoccupation with work, and an unusually competitive and aggressive attitude."[1] Type A women might interpret this list as assets for getting ahead. Indeed they are.

Type A types also exhibit quirks like speaking and eating quickly, and fidgeting, like foot tapping or playing with a pencil in a rhythmic fashion. They often dominate conversations and finish others' sentences.[2] My chatterbox "outer child" had grown up with that bad habit. I thought that demonstrated my gift for "just knowing" what others were thinking.

Unfortunately, these Type A behaviors can be more than quirky. They can be physically toxic. Just like the effects of smoking or hypertension, angry and hostile Type A behaviors have been linked to coronary problems.[3]

Type A people are pushed by time to achieve, while Type Bs take a more relaxed approach to deadlines, and ideally, to life. Once when I finished a speech about my Type A good girl work style, a young woman raised her hand, and asked, "What if I'm Type B?" Lucky, lucky girl. She's probably laid-back enough to rise to chairman of the board and still have a life.

Filling out this alphabet soup are "Type E women executives . . . who try to be Everything to Everyone." Researcher Waino W. Suojanen found that Type Es feel insecure and strive to believe in their personal worth while trying to meet the demands of home and work.[4] Whether women are competitive As, more laid-back Bs, or more pleasing Es, we can all grow to be Type T: tired from trying so hard.

Where Good Girls Come From

Patti Clark, president of coaching and consulting firm PS Clark & Associates in New Hope, Pennsylvania, defined good girls this way: "A good girl is a pleaser and wants to fit in." When Type A urgency is coupled with good girl tendencies, women can overdose on overdoing.

But Patti pointed to the consequences of the natural confidence-building messages that parents give good girls. Their encouragement instills the lifelong pursuit of approval. "Messages like, 'You can be on the best team and get the best grades,' trained women to believe that their fulfillment and happiness and all the good things in their lives came from external behavior and performances. These women then begin following what a parent or teacher or society said would be the 'road to success,' and doing everything 'right' over and over and over again." So good girls develop the habit of seeking approval that's never enough.

Dallas-based psychologist Dr. Kaye Moore agrees. "The difference between women and men is that women are inherently relational. Relationships are important to our emotional survival. Pleasing others becomes of paramount importance, so we're diligent about pleasing others and making relationships good so we feel good about ourselves."

In other words, from an early age, good girls learn to say "yes" as a way to secure relationships and get approval. Add Type A to that mix, and the urgency to please faster and better than anyone else lays a foundation for a work ethic than can verge on workaholism.

In this chapter, you'll meet women who moved from an A in school to A in ambition, eventually achieving wonderful things in their busy lives. But their embedded good behavior also earned them the stress of overworking and the pain of burning out. Most of these hardworking women began their pattern of people pleasing long before they hit the boardroom.

Were we born with this compulsion to achieve or did we do it to ourselves? How did this workaholic race begin?

Meet the Parents

Firstborn daughters are excellent candidates to be Type A good girls. I was one. So was Lisa K., a thirty-five-year-old marketer from Burlington, Vermont. She characterized herself as "the typical Type A firstborn daughter and overachiever. I was a good girl and I grew up with that Protestant work ethic that if you put your head down and you work really hard, someone will come over and pat you on the head and say, 'Good job.' "

Studies indicate that first-born girls are likely to grow up to become hardworking, highly responsible women. In his book, *Born to Rebel: Birth Order, Family Dynamics, and Creative Lives,* Frank Sulloway uses twenty-six years of research to paint the picture of firstborns as "self-assured, authoritarian conformists."[5] In a *Forbes* article about Sulloway's work, reporters Rita Koselka and Carrie Shook wrote that "female executives are much more likely to be firstborns than laterborns."[6] They add, "Sulloway's thesis is that firstborn children know that if life unfolds as it usually does, they will inherit the farm...To curry parental favor, they may become surrogate parents, bossy, responsible, and conscientious."[7]

Peggy, fifty-three, president of a nonprofit advertising group in New York City, was the oldest of fifteen children, whom she helped her mother raise. "I've been in management since I was five. I didn't resent it because the ability to help mom out at that level made me feel special. We were more like girlfriends." Approval leads to relationships leads to self-esteem.

While I met a number of firstborn daughters, they weren't the only Type A good girls. Whatever their birth order, good girls are the ones most attached to the expectations of parents, to whom they look for approval. They shine in the light of being loved for being good. Consciously or not, good girls' achievements became confused with parental approval. Mothers were key personal role models, while fathers often played hero roles.

Monique, forty-three, a high-powered editor of a national black women's magazine, is a great example. "I have always been a good girl. I have always wanted to make Momma proud. I was raised very modestly in Washington, D.C., by parents who did not have the privilege of going to college. I am the first in the generation of our last name to actually graduate."

Good girls look for the signals of a job well done and parental endorsement spurs even more effort. "I loved the fact that I got accolades from my parents when I achieved," said Donna D., forty-four, a Cincinnati-based consultant, who was once a corporate HR executive at Procter & Gamble. "From the time I entered the Girl Scouts and won the cookie-selling contest to being the captain of my basketball and softball teams, I was really looking for approval, and that 'Hey, way to go, kiddo.' I loved that my parents were always encouraging me to be the best I could be."

Being told "what a good girl you are" was a huge motivator for me, too. There's nothing as satisfying as being rewarded for good behavior by the people you love most.

Seeking approval as a child is natural. But, as adults, we see that desire can morph into a manic urge to please bosses and companies, even to the detriment of our own health and happiness. How does the simple yearning to be liked get so horribly out of control?

Many of the most accomplished women I met said that their accomplishments as adults finally made them feel like they had pleased their parents. When thirty-seven-year-old Lisa B.'s successful travel career went into overdrive, she thought back to the way she was raised. "My parents inspired me to be this driven." Then when it started to be too much, she said, "I was scratching my head, thinking, Wait a minute, isn't this what you wanted me to want?"

When thirty-four-year-old Courtney appeared in my doorway, this one-time dot-com entrepreneur had just taken a year off following a bankruptcy and divorce. She thought about why she put herself through so much. "Was it really for me or for my parents? Was I trying to prove something to them?" she wondered. "Once I achieved, and people liked what I did, I figured I've got to do more so they'll still like me."

Pleasing others, working hard, and getting ahead are all good behaviors. But where do we draw the line between good and good enough?

Good Inside and Out

Cheerfulness is a hallmark of "good girldom." Today, Rosemary, a forty-one-year-old childcare expert, still bubbles with girlish exuberance. Her upbeat personality masks the fact that she has survived being shot in a botched robbery and that the company she built has been undergoing big management changes. She described her little self as energetic and joyful. "My dad showed me a home movie of me as a toddler and I was always laughing. I was the kind of child who could've been in a garbage dump and it looked like fun. That's the child part of me that I see in myself as an adult. No matter where I am, I see the good side."

Though these women are not "Goody Two-shoes," they are well behaved. Camille, forty-four, a publicist, says, "I was a very good girl. I wanted to do the right thing. I never did drugs. I didn't rebel." Camille's childhood job was to be good.

Many took that job seriously. "I was always the worrier," says Kerry, thirty-three and a business owner in Vermont. "I worried about the school bus coming on time. I grew up on a farm, and when I had to go to school, I worried that my family wouldn't be able to run the farm without me."

Not everyone who ended up a good girl was born that way. Some grew into it. Listen to Ann, a forty-seven-year-old writer:

"Growing up, I was a conundrum. I appeared to be bright and to display leadership skills and be a hard worker. But there was another side. My teachers complained, 'If only she would pay attention, if only she would work.' I was the one who sat in the back of French lab listening to my Beatles tapes. I was thrown out of prep school in my senior year."

It took Ann till she was in her early twenties, when she faced the pressure to earn a living, to cast off the "conundrum" label and buckle down.

These little girl insecurities feed into adult perfectionism, different from the typical "dot the Is, cross the Ts" kind. We interpreted perfectionism as overdelivering on expectations, going above and beyond to do our over-the-top best. As we age, perfectionism can get in the way of our satisfaction, making some of us so brittle we snap. I would never describe myself as a perfectionist, but I would admit to being committed to making sure that jobs are done well, certainly well beyond what anyone ever asked of me.

Winning Is Good

Good girls like to win. The eldest in a family of four girls, Donata, now a forty-two-year-old home entertaining expert in California, brags, "We went from playing Miss America, where I always had to win, to playing army, where I was always the general."

"In the first grade, my mom sent me to ballroom dancing school," remembers Bonnie, fifty-one. "She wanted me to learn poise and thought that I would become a competitive dancer. I started competing all over the United States and by the time I was in second grade, I was a national champion for my age group." Bonnie eventually grew up to head marketing and sales for Continental Airlines.

My childhood, while wonderfully fun, was also a rehearsal for a grown-up career, at least that's the way I perceived it. My dad took a Dale Carnegie training course in public speaking. He would "present" to my brother and me when we were only five and six. We'd listen to him practice and then Jack and I would be expected to stand up and emote right back to him. Preparing for a winning work life was natural.

You Can Do Anything . . .

One phrase came up spontaneously in nearly every interview I had, and dozens of women phrased it nearly in these exact words: "My parents told me I could do and be anything I wanted to be." Growing up in the decades so influenced by the women's movement may have instigated our fixation on succeeding from an early age. We were taught that we should want to do it all and have it all, even before we knew what "it" was.

Lalita, who evolved from technology executive to author in her fifties, remembered hearing that same mantra. "My father thought I was smart and determined and that I could really make things happen. He always said, 'Whatever you want, you can do it.' There was just no limit to his dreams for me."

That prognosis for success came with an obligation to deliver. "My parents were high achievers and wanted us to do well," said Camille. "They instilled a ton of self-confidence in me. There was nothing we couldn't do. My father always said, 'It doesn't matter what you do, you have to be the best at it . . . if you're digging ditches, be the best ditch digger.' "

The "you can do anything" mantra is both a gift and a burden. We actually believed it, and in many cases, went far beyond anyone's expectations and boundaries. The burden? "You can do anything" implies that we have a limitless ability to do and achieve. It invites a lifetime of living up to our parents' belief in us.

Fear of disappointing parents is an underlying corollary of these high expectations. Debra, age forty-six, just started a sabbatical after twenty-five years of nonstop work. Her usually hard-charging "boss voice" is already softened with the gift of time and perspective. "In our house, if you got an A that was okay, but the underlying message was, 'Why didn't you get an A plus?' It was never good enough. My parents' expectations made me go that extra mile." Debra wasn't complaining. Like most good girls, she figured a little discipline was good for her.

Some families took the A standard too far. Lisa B. recalled her family's "grading technique" with chagrin: "Every house has a currency. Ours was not about being, but about doing. It wasn't enough to be pleasant or be authentic. How many jobs did I have? What was my GPA? What were my extracurricular activities? Because if I didn't have a bunch, my parents felt I was a loser or a quitter. When I stepped out of line, there wasn't a lot of forgiveness."

Donata put it this way, "On one hand, our parents were telling us, 'You can do anything.' On the other hand, in very subtle ways, they were making us feel loved if we brought home As. The goal was achieving, achieving, achieving."

Could we really be "anything" we wanted, or really any "good girl" thing we wanted? Did that "be anything" encouragement keep us believing we could and should, even though our adult world wouldn't be quite so supportive of our extraordinary expectations? Childcare options are still pretty dismal. Women still carry most of the "home work," even when they work outside the home. They continue to be paid less for the work they do. A 2001 survey revealed the continuing disparity with men, since on average, American women who work full-time, year round, earn 78 cents for every dollar earned by white men, the highest-earning group.[8]

No one told us that we might have to accomplish "everything we wanted" with less help, more demands, and fewer resources than any other generation. But good girls don't tend to ask for help. We try to prove we can do it all, and crave the affirmation that comes with it.

How does this good behavior—taking on multiple roles, demanding high standards, pleasing an ever-increasing number of others—manifest itself in adults? Debra L. Nelson and Ronald J. Burke, in an article from *The Academy of Management Executive*, say that "there is evidence that executive women experience over-load as a stressor, both in the form of role overload and total over-load. Role overload is the experience of competing or conflicting expectations from multiple roles, and women are particularly prone to this stressor."[9] Parenting, caring for others, being an employee and a good local citizen all pile on the role overload.

The authors go on to say that total overload is worse for women than men, since "research has indicated that women's average total workload was seventy-eight hours per week, where men's total workload was sixty-eight hours per week. The increased workload interfered with women's ability to effectively wind down, with resultant negative effects on health." Their study indicated that women age thirty-five to thirty-nine felt the greatest peak of work stress, as total workload increased with the number of children in the household.[10] Any mother of more than one child could affirm that study in a heartbeat.

With that as a background on the effects of too much Type A good girl behavior, why don't these talented, ambitious women try to choose professions that give them joy or at least stress relief? From a young age, we're encouraged to choose profit over passion.

Practical About Passion

Good girls learn early on to be practical. Our parents, and later teachers, counselors, and coaches were big factors in choosing the road more traveled.

Isa is a thirty-five-year-old Silicon Valley computer whiz who didn't start out to become a techno geek. "I played flute for a while, so I thought I'd grow up to be a musician. But my parents are very risk-averse people, and they wanted me to go to school for some-thing practical." Isa put aside her musical talents and focused on computer science. She worked for nearly ten years in the high-tech industry before she finally took a break and shaped a new life cen-tered in art and dance.

The pattern of making practical choices over passionate ones played out in many of my interviewees' lives. Raising a rock star wasn't exactly on the parenting agenda of most moms and dads. Ardith, despite her love of singing, worked her entire career in marketing. "Even while I was a buttoned-up businessperson, I always wanted to be Shawn Colvin." She hid it well. Not until Ardith stepped out of corporate life at forty did she resume her singing dreams.

Like many girls, I dreamed of making it on Broadway. Despite that, I remember my dad telling me that the theater would only be an "avocation" for me. He said that I should get a "real job" that would pay me for my talents. He was right to protect me from what would have been a challenging life at best, given my average talent. Instead, for twenty years, I succeeded at "legitimate" work before I went back to that avocation and began to speak onstage around the country, the closest I could get to that childhood passion.

Working Girls

Good girls are expected to earn our keep, so we identify with our careers from an early age. Kerry summed up it with this memory. "I had a Smurfette poster when I was in elementary school that said, 'Working Girl,' and I put it on my door."

New York–based marketer Joan, fifty, kept boosting her ambitions higher, predicting, "I was going to have a career I would love. I thought I wanted to be an actress or a director. When I got into my teens, I wanted to be a businesswoman on Wall Street."

Diana, forty-seven, who runs a custom publishing company in Boston, exposed her budding entrepreneurial roots and her ability to attract work. "From the time when I was nine or ten, I knew I wanted to own my own business. When most kids were playing doctor, I was playing 'office.' I would tape 'in' and 'out' boxes to my brother's door. My sister was the secretary. Thirty minutes into the game, they would throw all the work at me. The 'running the whole organization' thing really has always been in my blood."

Little girl career dreams even came with wardrobes. Monique recalled, "I decided I wanted to be a nurse because I was a fan of the TV show *Julia*, who was the first professional black woman on television. My mother got me a nurse outfit."

"I was going to be a geriatrician," laughed Donata. "I adore old people. I would wear my white coat and my stethoscope and everyone would be acknowledging me, 'Dr. Donata this, Dr. Donata that.' I always look really good in my daydreams."

Courtney cast herself as a well-dressed diva with fancy digs. "I had dreams of being a *Cosmopolitan* cover girl with a loft in New York with brick walls and wood floors. I always imagined I would walk into the corporate offices, Miss High Heels, climbing my way up the ladder." Courtney's imagined scene became a reality.

These women had fully dressed dreams that even extended to their kids. Showing just how much control she expected to exert on her future, Julie, age thirty-six, a principal in a Washington, D.C.–based consulting firm, thought she would grow up to be a married lawyer or a judge with 2.5 kids who would wear OshKosh overalls and color-coordinated little turtlenecks.

Nine-to-Five Fever

Type A good girls are eager to begin their careers right out of school. By then, we're ready for independence and a larger stage.

Some set their fates even before they graduated. Kerry laughed, "In the high school yearbook, you had to predict where you would be in five years. I wrote, 'I will be a major executive looking out of the corner office, ordering around my male secretary.' Seven years later, I had the corner office and my male administrative assistant put that clipping on my desk." Kerry felt so embarrassed, especially since she'd recently been an assistant herself.

Peri, age forty-five, a Chicago-based media executive, was in career overdrive before she turned twenty. "I started in the ad business at nineteen so I didn't have college as a formative time," she says wryly. "My father was in the business, as were my friends. At twenty-two, I was a VP on big national accounts. I figured out life working in advertising."

Media images of glamorous working women became reflected in reality. "Remember that movie *Working Girl*?" asked Courtney. "The theme song was my inspiration. I'd be jogging around the World Trade Center in the morning and I'd hear 'Let the River Run' in my head. I'd run alongside the Hudson River, mentally shouting to the passing ferryboats, Here we are! We're all working!" (Several years later, when Courtney survived bankruptcy and divorce, she changed her tune. "When I ran, I'd think of that song again and I'd mutter, 'That river can just keep going on without me!' ")

Type A good girls bring incredible energy and enthusiasm even to their entry level jobs. No job is too small not to matter. Donna D. recalled, "In college, I worked twenty to twenty-five hours a week. I loved being the intramural commissioner and the athletic director's secretary. I went right from college three weeks later to join Procter & Gamble. No break."

Loving work is a characteristic of good girls who succeed. Listen to Santa Monica resident Liz, forty-six, describe her love for what might have been a mundane part-time job as a telephone information operator on campus: "I just loved the combination of having my finger on the pulse of what was going on that night and the detective work involved in finding people, well before computers. If they asked for a nameless someone who lived in a certain part of the campus who was from New Jersey, I would say, 'Call me back in fifteen minutes!' " Liz eventually became the wise and wisecracking second sister of the *Satellite Sisters* national radio talk show.

Emboldened through good grades and their teenage work experiences, women took their overachieving ethos to the office. They transformed setbacks into opportunities.

Here's Monique's story. "I graduated at the top of my class, and I began my career at Fairchild Publications in a one-year minority training program. Even at that time, folks said, 'Why do you need a minority training program, why can't you go in and be a reporter?' But I always look for opportunity. I was doing obits and the small stories that a freshman reporter gets. On my own time, I wrote a piece on the importance of the black consumer to the fashion industry. I turned it in, saying, 'If you like it, fine. If not, just tell me how it can be improved.' It won an award for the newspaper, so they took me off the training program in two months' time." Monique would eventually become editor in chief of *Essence* magazine.

Good girls also know how to spin the wrong job into the right one. When Liz accepted the plum job as the head of PR for Cartier in the United States, her first day at work unfortunately coincided with some bad news in October of 1987. "I was sitting in the chairman's office when the stock market dropped five hundred points. That was very bad for business in the superhigh end of luxury products. All week long, all kinds of very expensive pieces of jewelry were returned. I started to hatch a plan that would get me out of New York." That case of bad timing led her to head public relations for an upstart company in Oregon called Nike.

Riveted on Getting It Right

Some women tried to pursue careers that were offshoots of their inherent "goodness." A true Type A, thirty-nine-year-old Pam's interest in helping people led her to a degree in psychology. "I went straight on to grad school and did a master's in clinical social work in the inner city. But I was so drained and frustrated with the slow rate of the patients' improvement that I just wanted to say to them, 'Snap out of it!' " This frustration is a typical Type A response. She turned her psychology interests to marketing instead. "I decided to shift gears toward helping people through health care—related communications. It seemed like a more altruistic kind of marketing."

Though Julie got a dose of early "military training" by spending a semester cleaning guns in the Israeli army, she moved to Chad to join the Peace Corps. "I wanted to change the world and still believed I could bring democracy and make people's lives better."

Like Cinderellas, women switched jobs like trying on slippers, hoping to find not only the one that fit, but the one they loved. I found a way to use my first Avon job to get the one I really wanted. Once I became the editor of the newsletter, I decided it would be a great way to interview everyone I could possibly want to work with in the company. One of those stories led to my first copywriting job. Like other good girls, I was never without an agenda.

One characteristic that plagues good girls is that we never settle. There's either a better job, or a more fulfilling one. And we are willing to uproot or miss out on the fun parts of our twenties or work like dogs to get it. Any job worth doing is worth doing better.

Welcome to the Club

How do you know if you're a good girl, still pulsing with work ethic and the need to achieve and please? Whether you were born that way, raised that way, or became one in retaliation, you know it, just as you know you're tall or you're someone who blushes. The worksheet that ends this chapter might confirm your suspicions.

The Type A gene determines the pace of our accomplishments and the heights of the workload we assume. The good girl DNA assures that we never say "no" until it's nearly too late and that we often worry more about everyone else's happiness, and their approval and love which we believe will come along with it, than our own. Type A good girls are probably the best-loved people in the office or in the car pool. Our inner fire can light up a room. But what happens when the candle burns out?

The combination of the urge to win and achieve with the desire to please and do the right thing creates a powerful life force. That inborn good girl conviction inflames our decisions, our ambitions, and eventually our lives. We are tenacious about our goals and expectations. We are often our own worst bosses, because as much as we expect of the world, it's nothing compared to what we expect of ourselves.

Fortunately, our first real work experiences are generally positive. First jobs lead to promotions and recognition that feeds our hunger for more. During the early years, it doesn't hurt to be a Type A good girl. In fact, it's a formula for success.

Never Good Enough

I don't think that many of us realized that we were taking our childhood attitudes and hopes to the office. Our urge to achieve and to please is our good girl credential for success. We may even feel offended that the good girl syndrome might be a precursor to burnout. We like the image of ourselves as the can-do go-getters.

Every time we worked hard to get the next carrot, we quickly set another goal. Good girls see work achievements as the validation that we are doing what we were meant to do in the world. That we're not squandering the talents we were given. Why rest when there is so much we can do?

I remember back to my own grade school experience when the nuns would admonish the girls with the best grades, "Don't rest on your laurels." For years, I thought "laurels" meant "elbows." But the effect was the same. The job of a good girl is to be better and to do more, not to rest or congratulate herself. More, more, more. Taking a break was never a consideration or a desire.

When we couple the energy and ambition of our early years with our eager-to-please, over-the-top performance, we begin a pattern of overworking that can stick with us for life. Early on, we don't notice its debilitating effects on our personal lives. It's only after several years—or, for some women, a couple of decades—of trying too hard and caring too much, that we learn that we've got to give our good girl selves a rest.

Profile of a Good Girl: Rosemary's Story

One of the hallmarks of being a good girl is the identification with parents' approval and the desire to do the right thing. Rosemary's story is an example of how that identification can be so intense and lasting that it can provide the strength not only to do and be good, but to make a life change.

Rosemary, now forty-one, is the oldest of three children and her good behavior was her trademark. "I was the perfect daughter through the eighth grade. My work ethic was defined very early and that has served me well. Even in the worst of circumstances, I can hear my mom saying, 'Whatever you're doing, do it well.'" In Rosemary's case, "well" translated to being the best, reaching for more, being the 100 percent girl.

"My mother was the key influence in my career. She didn't work outside the home and didn't have a college degree," she said lovingly. "She just lived life authentically, with no airs about her. She was a deeply faithful person. She graduated first in her class in high school but because she was a girl, she was asked to go to work so her brothers could go to college. Her family, recently immigrated, had traditional expectations."

Her mother transferred her own dreams of education and success to Rosemary. "When Mom dropped me off at Wellesley, she took me aside and said, 'You are going to be able to do whatever you want to do with this education, but be sure that whatever you choose to do, you are passionate about.'" That became the cornerstone of her life. She felt she was "called" to do something important.

She created a company dedicated to creating childcare solutions in partnership with corporations and developed a reputation as a visionary in the area of childcare. "For eleven years, I led this organization in a way my mother would be so proud to see. I have found a way to have my work really express what I value."

Her mother's death was particularly difficult for her. "When my mother died, the shine went out of my world," said Rosemary. She buried herself in her work.

Her mother's death was the first of several setbacks that taught

Rosemary about the hard realities of life. Her sunny outlook masks her inner worries about the media myths that young women buy into, that having a successful working life is easy and without pain.

"The examples that are put in front of young women in college are women being successful: 'Ta-dah, here's your success!' Nobody talks about the very jagged edge. I had to confront mortality at a very young age."

She continued, "My mother died when I was young. Then my sister was very sick. When my sister was going through chemo, I learned it was such a privilege to care for somebody who is suffering because you may think you are giving, but you are getting. But now I have a sense of urgency. The clock is running out and I feel like I can't squander the time. Maybe I would feel differently if I didn't have that sense of 'Wow, it could happen any moment.' "

If those two losses weren't enough to convince Rosemary to really live her life, her own near-death experience in a botched store robbery drove the message home. "I got hit by two of the gunman's shots. I tried to run and I couldn't, so I hid behind the back of a car." Unfortunately, the car was the robber's and he came after her.

"He pointed the gun at my head. My life went in front of my eyes. It felt like it took ten hours and it was probably ten seconds. I got this image in my mind. I was little and my mother was ironing and I was ironing with my toy iron next to her. She was there with me, which made me feel so calm. I knew he wasn't going to shoot me and I looked at him and said, 'I am so sorry that this all went wrong.' " The man just stared at Rosemary, then ran away.

Rosemary, who was sympathetic to the robber because he was in this "botched" situation, represents the all-time good girl. How many of us say an automatic "I'm sorry" for everything, rather than cast blame, in order to make everything all right? Good girls do it all the time.

Afterward, the shooting really hit home. "I thought of that quote from <u>The Brothers Karamazov</u> . . . 'One good memory in your child-hood may one day be your salvation.' " That's exactly how I felt. I couldn't go to work for a week because I didn't want people to see me so rattled. It was the most reflective week of my life. Every moment I felt the presence of my mother and the experience really defined me in this parochial sense: I know what I have the ability to be and shame on me if I don't live up to it. Her voice urged, 'Do not screw up your life!' "

After surviving these difficulties, Rosemary redoubled her efforts to make her work reflect her values. "I was very clear: If I can't be exactly who I am every day, I have to leave."

The new management group was the turning point for change. Like a good girl, she gave their new direction a shot, but found herself acting against her beliefs. "I tried for a year to see if I could reconcile those feelings, but I couldn't," she said. "The reality is I wouldn't choose to leave, but my work was no longer bringing out the best in me."

Coincident with this business circumstance, Rosemary met Billy, and they got engaged. That gave her another reason to step away from her role as leader. She is taking the next year off to consider her future, while enjoying her new marriage. "I didn't want to begin a marriage in disequilibrium. My passion for my work is within me and that passion will go with me. It will come out again in the next thing I do. Billy has given me the confidence to see it was not just chance that drove my success. It will happen again. The joy is transferable, the passion is transferable."

While some women might think that getting married is not the time to change careers, but to retain some independence and stability, Rosemary looked at it differently. "It took me twenty years to find this man and I think of work in the same way. It's like a love.

You can fake yourself out or you can tolerate dating just for the sake of having company. You do work for the sake of having your paycheck but there's a difference in having a passion and the love of your life, and I don't want to accept anything less than the love of my life."

Is finding the perfect job as elusive as finding the perfect soul mate? Are we setting ourselves up for disappointment if we set our expectations so high? As good girls, we never stop shooting for 100 percent. We don't know how to think in terms that are halfhearted or good enough. Rosemary is spending the next year searching for what's next in her life. "Everyone keeps coming to me with ideas. It's more important to me to be in the company of people who aspire for more profound changes for children. But I am clear in my conviction to not just do something for the sake of doing something. I have faith I will know the right thing when it presents itself. Everything I did before, all the bruises, makes me stronger for what's next."

FINDING YOUR INNER GOOD GIRL

Picture yourself or, better yet, find a photograph of yourself from your early good girl days and put it in this frame. This is your good girl reference point.

As you look at or recall this image of yourself, can you see any early indicators of your Type A-ness? _____

_____

_____

Do you look happy, worried, anxious, hopeful? _____

_____

Who loved this child best? _____

Has anyone else in your life ever given you that same unwavering love or approval? _____

_____

Fill in the blank: When I was young, I was more _____ than I am now. _____

Relative to that quality, what has changed? _____

_____

_____

What has stayed the same? _____

Do you want that quality back in your life now? _____

What would it take to get it back? _____

_____

What advice would you give this little girl knowing what you know now? _____

_____

_____

Who were you before life took its toll? _____

_____

_____

_____

_____

CHAPTER THREE

Working Hard, Feeling the Burn

In a book that's all about what happens when women work too hard, there is a sunny side to the story: Women love to work. Work can be fun, satisfying, and energizing, if managed properly. A survey by nonprofit research group Catalyst reveals that 67 percent of women in dual-career marriages would continue working whether or not they needed the money."[1]

Hard work can actually be healthy for us. A study from *The Academy of Management Executive* reported that "the evidence indicates that work in general actually has positive effects on women's health. Employed women have better health than unemployed women in terms of fewer sick days, better psychological well-being, and greater resilience to family role stress."[2] The study assumes that this "healthy work" includes "support and encouragement, challenging jobs, the absence of stressful conflict, a balanced workload, and clear expectations."[3] That's likely the dream list of every working woman.

I don't mean to sugarcoat the tedium of work, especially when many women are in a hand-to-mouth, dead-end job. But during our lives, most of us fortunately have a job or two where we can't wait to start the day. The luckiest among us have lifetime careers we love. Women's ambitions run high, with 55 percent of female senior executives wanting the top job in their company and another 19 percent have not ruled it out.[4]

Money and titles are not the only motivation. The most loved jobs intersect passions, talents, and values. While this might define a great job for anyone, it's especially satisfying for Type A good girls because our full-throttle work style is paid off in personal satisfaction.

I keenly felt that personal satisfaction in one of my Avon roles. The Avon sales managers suffered the same difficulties as other salespeople. They were often on the road alone, looking for the next recruit while trying to deal with all the headquarters communication, so I came up with a way to simplify the process.

Once a month, I recorded a simple audio tape, a blend of encouragement and tips to simplify their meetings. As the managers were driving to sales calls, my voice kept them company. By listening to me "act out" their script, they could do it without rehearsal. Their relieved feedback told me that what I did mattered.

Growing up as a Type A good girl was great preparation for the world of work. Our work ethic breeds the ultimate résumé: Hardworking, seeks to exceed boss's expectations, wants to do the right thing, loyal, impatient for results, positive disposition, sets high goals. We are the women that employers covet. We are the women who care so much about excellence that we will strive for it even to the detriment of our own health and happiness.

Whether it was intentional or not, the success strategy I heard from most good girls translated to all work and hardly any play. Work hard, ask for more, work harder, want more. Their wins masked the many sacrifices in their personal lives, but in the beginning, it was all about getting ahead. We don't win many kudos for the normal stuff of life, like playing with our dogs or picnicking in the park.

Get Ahead or Bust

Isa was an example of Type A urgency to get ahead. After graduating with a degree in computer science, Isa found no takers for her talents. She accepted a job as an assistant in a law firm as a holding measure. She said, "I couldn't get a job in the computer industry to save my life." Isa secretly believed, If I just work harder, they'll recognize me.

Isa finally landed a computer spot, but seventeen months into her next job, she was frustrated. She said to her manager, "This is not challenging anymore. Either give me more work or I need to find another job." Success added up to, "Okay, next?"

Sometimes hard work just begets more work. Erika Brown, a life coach in Denver, Colorado, commented, "I think women honestly think that if you just keep working harder, there's always more you can do. A guy will say, 'There's nothing more I can do.' A woman will internally say, I must not be good enough, so I've got to change and I've got to work harder."

Thanks to their good-sport nature, women welcome hard work as a challenge, despite the price. Lisa K. got a job with a major consumer products company, along with a handpicked handful of undergrads from across the country. "We got six months to sink or swim," said Lisa. "But I wouldn't call it swimming. I worked my butt off. Typically, when you start off your career, you're working crazy hours. You're putting every ounce of physical and emotional energy into your career because that's what you need to do."

There's a tendency among these women to get their energy from the thrill of overcoming adversity or others' doubts. Donna D. linked her persistence to her sports training. "I always had this determination. I was going to get promoted. I was going to do a great job. There was nothing like the thrill of winning when people said you couldn't win. I blew out my knee in my junior year of high school and they said I'd never play college basketball. I became captain of my team. You tell me I can't do it, and I do it . . . just to show you."

Every Minute Counts

Before long, the excessive hours become the proof of dedication. "Singlemindedness is why I advanced in the early years," asserts Ardith, who took a severance package after she hit forty and moved to Santa Fe. "Back then, If I'd left the office at five-thirty, I don't know if I'd have been able to do what I do now. In the early days, work was more fun. It was a social thing to come in on a Saturday. I didn't resent it."

The fever to achieve rises when coworkers and friends are equally obsessed. One former advertising executive remembers working some nights till 2:00 or 3:00 in the morning, "but most of my friends were doing the same thing in our twenties and early thirties. We worked long and crazy high-pressure hours. Our families never understood how anyone ever worked like that." Late-night hours become the badge of honor for the overcommitted few.

I, too, felt it was natural to work long hours in my first jobs. When I was twenty-two, the long hours were the price of getting ahead. Somewhere there's a secret success code that suggests that we get to work earlier than the boss, and leave after he or she goes home. The long hours were tied to approval, and to "not disappointing." If I got in after my boss, I was shamefaced. In some companies, overtime is part of the drinking water. But good girls will burn the midnight oil even in low-key firms. They don't know how to slack off.

While postcollege years are natural breeding grounds for overtime, these women acknowledged that their excessive work energy lasted long past their twenties. Joan described a ritual of hectic days even into her forties. She'd start at 8:15 A.M. before others got in "because I liked the calm before the storm." Her day would extend to 7:00 or 7:30 P.M. and she'd never leave without the next day's to-do list completed. She admitted that she was compelled to work in high-pressure jobs. "If I ever wrote an autobiography, it would be titled *Attracted to Chaos.* Knowing I had that list was my way of coping with all the chaos that was around me, which fed me and gave me all my energy." Addiction to busyness is a characteristic I observed again and again.

Joan's pattern of starting the workday early was a common thread. Certainly, that extra early hour can be a calming ritual to begin the day with some semblance of control, but it becomes another eroding factor that lengthens women's days. Early morning also could be spent exercising or reading or just doing nothing. Soon, the rest of the day converts to work time. Evenings become the perfect time to read e-mails. Sunday nights seemed destined for pre-Monday worrying. Why rest when you can work or worry about working?

Every minute counts. Time on the job is productive and even fun. But the obsession with filling every minute with a to-do list begins a pattern of thinking of time off as lazy time—in other words, time that could have been used to get ahead, to earn more. Ironically, over time, working hours actually begin to feel comfortable . . . and resting hours uneasy.

Sylvia Gearing, Ph.D., a clinical psychologist experienced in women's issues, was the first to coin the term "female executive stress syndrome," or FESS, about the distressed female executive who seems to have it all but is stressed-out and close to burnout. Among the characteristics Dr. Gearing discovered were three related to their time-on/time-off attitudes. FESS women would rather be at work than at home, they see work as an escape, and they equate performance with love.[5] While FESS is more likely to strike in midcareer, it's easy to see how an early pattern of work without time off can accelerate this outcome.

The Workaholics Anonymous website lists questions to help determine when work has gotten out of hand. "Do you take work with you to bed, on weekends, on vacation? Is work the activity you like to do best and talk about most?"[6] Obviously, too many yeses aren't good news.

A couple of the women I met learned to draw lines between their long work hours and their personal lives. Omaha-born Kay, now forty-six, worked as a trial lawyer in a New York firm where huge numbers of billable hours were legendary. "It was the eighties and law firms really abused associates," Kay said. "Some nights, I literally worked around the clock, just like cannon fodder, proofreading big documents. I have always liked to work hard, but I do not like to work on Saturday nights. Midwestern people are hardworking, but the whistle blows at five o'clock and you go home. I just feel like, you don't own me."

Fast Times on the Fast Track

Our obsession with performance and time urgency is a key weapon in a fast-track career. Ardith propelled herself through her early years. "I graduated from Wellesley in '82 and then worked a year at the Benton & Bowles ad agency, before going to business school. I wanted to get an MBA as fast as I could, so I got one from Northwestern in '85." Her rapid-fire rise continued in marketing, then consulting, then ten years at Clairol. "I joined as a product manager, was promoted in two months, and then to group product manager. Then I was responsible for U.S. haircolor, then international VP of marketing, and finally chief innovation officer." Her stature and salary were the payoff for jet-fueled good behavior.

Kerry credited her swift rise in public relations to her aggressive energy. "I got my cluelessness out of the way in my internships. I hit the ground running after college. I knew I wanted to get promoted. I was sprinting to the finish line. I didn't wait for people to ask me to do things. I didn't want to be a financial drain to my parents, so making money was part of that and I was always trying to work one level above me." Kerry sought that over-her-head sensation. Her fast-track results? "I became a vice president of a PR agency at twenty-four, the youngest in the history of the company. At twenty-five, I looked around and said, 'What's my next step?' "

When I interviewed women about their career paths, they ticked off the titles and promotions—in other words, "what they did." It was harder to get them to talk about how they felt or what the job meant to them on a personal level. Getting ahead was job one.

When my mentor and longtime Avon friend Diane, now fifty-nine, accepted a secretarial job in advertising, she bumped into the wall of parental disapproval. "They said, 'We didn't spend all this money to send you to college so you could become a secretary.' " So Diane figured out a way to get promoted. She drafted letters under her boss's signature to save him work. As a reward, he told her to sign her own name, which triggered her promotion to account director. From there, Diane was in a rapid rise to the top.

Listening to these early career stories is like pacing a racehorse. Why were we in such a hurry to succeed? I believe it's because we love to work. We're good at it. We're rewarded for it. We are more conscientious than conscious. We don't see the risks of creating a life that's "always on."

The price of "always on" is that we never stop to take the restorative breath that can help us keep running. Several of the experts I interviewed called on lessons they'd learned from Tony Schwartz's book *The Power of Full Engagement*. Alicia Whitaker, global head of training and development at Credit Suisse, was one of them. "The basic concept people learn is that stress is not a bad thing. Top performance often comes about because you are stressing yourself and pushing yourself to maximum capacity. But the way it works is to think of a series of sprints, periods of stress with periods of recovery, not as a marathon."

Lucky to Do It All

A lot of Type A good girls use the word "lucky" to explain their quick ascent. They apply luck to their speedy promotions and their successes. They credit the serendipity of being at the right place at the right time and take for granted how hard they work. Monique, who was managing a bed-and-breakfast while simultaneously editing a national magazine and raising her young daughter, said, "I never thought to give up one thing for the other. I'm very passionate about all that I do and I've always been a multitasker. I just thought I would keep adding all the things that make me happy and I never thought about subtracting any."

Career coach Patti Clark assesses the multitasking from this seasoned perspective: "Creative, talented people don't know when to stop creating. They're so good at creating, they're energized by it. They live in expansion . . . not by cutting back. It may be because they never feel like they do enough." It's also a matter of not giving credit to ourselves for the many things we pull off. After a big success, Patti said it's not uncommon to hear, "Oh, that's nothing. Oh, I built a building . . . I forgot about that."

Women's organic comfort with multitasking contributes to our ability to take on more. According to the Families and Work Institute, 45 percent of American workers think they are asked to do too many tasks at once.[7] However, recent studies have shown that the consequence of modern multitasking, like reading your email while you talk on the phone, is the slow erosion of our ability to think and process information. As Sue Shellenbarger writes in *The Wall Street Journal*, "a growing body of scientific research shows . . . multitasking can actually make you less efficient, and, well, stupider. Trying to do two or three things at once or in quick succession can take longer overall than doing them one at a time, and may leave you with reduced brainpower to perform each task."[8] In other words, we are blasting away precious brain cells while we do too many things at once. It's a penalty women unconsciously pay since they can't stop doing it.

Another contributor to eventual burnout is the feeling that we need to do it all. Good girls maintain the self-deception that "only I can do a job right." The problem is ego, pure and simple. We fear doing less than 100 percent and worse, saying no or disappointing someone. Good girls get so used to pleasing that we develop an inability to tolerate that queasy feeling when a client says, "You're not coming?" We need to practice allowing ourselves to live with that twinge of guilt. The feeling is uncomfortable, but it passes.

Despite their overactive work ethic, good girls rarely congratulate themselves for all their achievements. Donna G., forty-four, leads marketing efforts for a wrestling promoter. She recalled her early working years this way: "I just kept getting promoted. I didn't know why, but I guess I was good. I knew I was working really, really hard."

The pattern of quietly working away without credit (either from a boss or from within yourself) can lead to bitterness under stress. I've heard women rant, "Don't they realize all I'm doing?" as they near the exhaustion point. Maybe "they" don't know. Good girls aren't good at bragging or complaining even when the going gets tough. That's why they are so appealing to work with.

The realization that we have made it sometimes sneaks up on us. We take our own value for granted. Diane said, "After graduation, I thought I would work in New York City for a couple of years, then get married, move back to Long Island, and be president of the PTA." Instead, Diane worked through nearly twenty years of promotions. "I was sitting in a meeting with the head of communications, who was probably about forty-five, but to me he was this older guy. And I was his boss. And all of a sudden, it hit me. I don't have a job. I had a career."

Loyal and True

The longer women stay, the harder it can be to even think about stepping away. Loyalty to their companies and jobs is another good girl trait. Diane and I share the tendency of identifying with the place we work as if we're rooting for the home team. It's not an "act," it's a true affinity and belief in the values of the people we signed on to support. Diane has told me that no matter where she worked, she believed in the company 100 percent.

Loyalty to others kept me in my office chair longer than I wanted to be. How could I leave all the people I cared about, all the people who depended on me? My job wasn't to walk out or admit burnout. My role was to lead with the most positive, enduring smile in the corridor. But the effort to always be the "up" person at work takes its toll.

Donna G., who has yet to take any time off, described her day-to-day coping method as "the ability to go with the flow. I try to be a positive, good person. I have the ability to say that I enjoy my work, even when I'm having the worst day in the whole world. Perhaps it's being phony, not most of the time, but when you have to."

Many good girls aren't willing to be that honest. Even when the work pressure gets out of hand, it's easier to give the manic "everything's wonderful" response and hope that tomorrow will improve. For most of my working years, I truly was happy most of the time. Whenever anyone asked me how I was doing at work, I always burst out with, "Great!" (with multiple exclamation points). Over time, though, when the job got more tiring and difficult, I'd still answer "great" when asked. It was a reflex, but also a protection against admitting the alternative. Refusing to acknowledge that anything could possibly be wrong is vintage good girl and that's why some women are blindsided when the love affair with overwork breaks down.

Losing Track

The evolution from hard-charging, Type A, working good girl to tired, stressed-out defector is gradual. The fixation on getting ahead and taking care of others' needs distracts us from the deterioration of our personal lives. As their agendas heated up, women told me what slowly dropped off their schedules. Time with friends. Time to exercise. Time to have an uninterrupted vacation with the family. Time to sleep.

These effects of work stress are not imagined. According to Dr.

Naomi Swanson, supervisory research psychologist at the National Institute for Occupational Safety and Health, "women are more likely to experience difficulty sleeping, nervousness, headaches, nightmares, lack of motivation. They are more likely to report mental health symptoms, like anxiety and depression, than men." That stress unfortunately leads to other reactive behaviors in women. "They smoke a bit more, and we find more reports of eating disorders."

Rather than take care of ourselves or seek help from friends and family, we turn to cell phones and computers as trusted companions. Weekends blur into the postwork week Friday crash and the Sunday preweek preparation. So many women have told me of their sleepless Sunday nights. The daily time clock can tick into years of sleepwalking through your real life so that it's hard to see what's really happening. Our fixation on the fast track makes us lose track of our lives.

I remember one incident when my husband, Joe, and I finally took a long weekend in New England. I was on the phone with the office from taxi to tarmac and finally to a seaside inn. Our room wasn't ready, so we waited outside. While Joe took in the spectacular ocean view, I was arguing over some client issue that I can't even remember now. There were kids playing nearby, so I raised my voice to keep my cell phone "meeting" going. Frustrated, Joe stalked away. When I finally got off the phone twenty minutes later, he wheeled on me. "Did you know how loud you were? Do you even realize we are at a vacation place? Do you see what you're becoming?" I didn't. I thought I was doing my job.

We lose track of priorities as the combination of personal and professional obligations gets overwhelming. "I have always used the analogy of the guy who had the act where he had all those plates in the air, and one would topple and he'd run and get that one going again, and another would topple," said Karen J., fifty-two, industrial show producer, wife of Paul, mom of Sophie. "Once you throw a child into the equation, it's just more plates falling down."

These feelings of being overwhelmed are conditioned behaviors, says Dr. Kaye Moore, who counsels many moms. "Girls get an unwritten message that self-sacrificing and putting others before themselves is absolutely what women do. If you interview women and ask, 'What did it feel like to you to have a mother who put everyone in front of herself?' they answer, 'I hated it,' because their mothers were resentful and irritable a lot of time. Yet, as adults, they are replicating what they saw. It's like software, it gets ingrained."

Putting Off Real Life

Gradually, the normal activities like eating, spending time with friends, and exercising fall off the must-do list. Lisa B. refused to allow "nonwork" items to interfere with her day. She'd get to the office by 7:00 A.M., so that she'd get some quiet time. She'd attend five or six meetings, sit in on a couple of conference calls, and answer an average of seventy-five to 150 e-mails a day and another forty voice mails. Lisa recalled, "Maybe somebody would try to interrupt me with, 'Let's get together, it's so-and-so's birthday,' and I'd think, Oh, just give her the damn cake to get it over with."

Even Lisa's dog missed out on her attention. "I was working till eight or nine at night, but I was supposed to be at doggie day care by seven to get my dog. I was always the last 'parent' to get there, and she was just hanging out there by herself."

As much as I wanted a dog during my advertising years, Joe resisted. "The dog would die of constipation if it had to wait for you to get home," he said. He was right. Work came first.

Normal respites like eating dinner disappear with the increased devotion to work. Lalita, perhaps a typical Silicon Valley workhorse, said, "I was working anywhere from sixty to eighty hours a week. I had squeezed every activity out of my life that didn't contribute to my job. I was no longer exercising. Somebody delivered my meals to the front door in Tupperware containers. There was an evening where I walked upstairs with my containers, popped the lid, and started eating. I never sat down. I never turned on the lights. I was so tired, I just went to bed. I thought, This has gotten very sick."

Day by day, small postponements stretch into critical lifetime decisions. I've heard younger women decide their wedding dates based on the fiscal calendar. One young woman pulled me aside after a speech and tearfully asked me if having a baby would take her out of the running for a promotion. I know of women who have induced labor so they could give birth while they were on Christmas vacation.

Over the course of a working lifetime, we can slip into an unconsciousness about our personal world, and develop an intense attachment to our busy world. When we love what we do, it's easy to let our personal needs take a backseat. Good girls often don't see the need to stop and take care of themselves because they are so busy pleasing everyone else.

You've Got to Have Friends

I asked women to think back over the bumps that led to the burn and one of the most familiar signs is losing touch with the people who love you most.

Lisa B. recalled the slow erosions of her friendships and family relationships. "I wish I would have noticed all the thousands of bad decisions I made, like barely coming home for the holidays or forgetting friends' birthdays or being unavailable for weddings. I'd resent that I had to give up my free time to be there. My friends suddenly became obstacles."

Lalita recalled that before she left Sun Microsystems, she didn't have time for her friends, and "the people I knew were more acquaintances, people you get information from. The contact was more about usefulness. It was just all too efficient."

Human resources expert Marcia Worthing suggested that friends are one of the key links to keeping a balanced view of work and life. Yet they are often the first to go as the burnout progresses.

"A friendship takes a lot of time, like touching base, or exchanging e-mails, or phone calls, and the little gifts at certain times. And when women get into these pressure zones, the friendships go when they're needed the most."

Marcia recalled a personal situation where her own friends intervened. "I have my two best friends in California, and I hadn't seen them for a couple of years. I was in San Jose and asked them to dinner. And they came and they said, 'You are violating our friendship. You are not taking this seriously enough. You are too much into your job.' It was a huge wake-up call for me."

If our agenda since childhood is to work hard, do a good job, and get ahead, good girls easily drop the details of normal life, like eating well, exercising, or sleeping. In the early years, bursting with naïveté and sheer love of working, we fill our plates because we can. But over time, our diminishing personal lives start to weigh us down. Most days, we get over the rough spots because we have to. We need the job or we want the self-esteem or perks that come with it. We figure that it's called work for a reason.

When Is Enough Enough?

The signs of burnout are clearer in the rearview mirror. Good girls are skilled at denying that problems exist. They turn a blind eye, hoping that eventually things will work out. Even the word "burnout" is anathema, like getting an F for failure. Maybe "worn out" is a better term. Sometimes you just wear out. And until you step out of your day-to-day agenda, you can't even see how much you needed a break to restore yourself.

The physiological symptoms of burnout might be harder to ignore than the social or job-related ones. Dr. Redford Williams, director of the Behavioral Medicine Research Center at Duke University Medical Center, talked of the differences between women and men. "Women are more prone to respond in chronic stress by becoming depressed, where men are more likely to get angry. Feeling overwhelmed, depressed, hopeless, helpless, caught, these are pretty good warning signs [for women]."

One of the most debilitating effects of burnout is that we can't even escape in sleep. Dr. Williams describes it this way: "Waking up or waking up early, or not being able to fall asleep, or reliving the day's events is often a sign of anxiety. You can't get them out of your head. Waking up early in the morning, at three or four A.M., having difficulty getting back to sleep, that's very often a sign of depression."

As a charter member of the "3:00 A.M. Wake-up Club," staring at the digital clock and conducting the "what ifs" of my next day, I know I fit Dr. Williams's profile. I didn't realize that was a precursor to depression.

Fatigue, lack of exercise, vacations attached to a cell phone, these are the more obvious signs of burnout, but there are some hidden symptoms. The urgency to work makes good girls unwilling to stop work for anything, even going to the bathroom. As personal as that sounds, many of the women resisted even a trip down the hallway. A small, personal break was an intrusion into their day. No wonder the "expendable" choices, like their friendships, went by the wayside.

We work hard because we have to and we want to, but also because we need to feel needed and indispensable. We get hooked on the pace and the rewards and just the busyness of it all. We lose track of how long it's been since we've had a good night's sleep, let alone a morning when we couldn't wait to wake up and charge in to do it all over again. Why does it have to get so bad before we make our lives good again?

Anatomy of Burning Out: Courtney's Story

Courtney was the quintessential Internet entrepreneur of the late nineties. An easy socializer with a theatrical bent, she created a business of hosting parties called Cocktails with Courtney in New York's Silicon Alley to bring together investors, advertisers, and technology innovators. A writer and publisher, she chronicled the events in her own newsletter called The Cyber Scene. For four years, before the bubble burst, she had a sexy, skyrocketing career as "the Contessa of Tribeca."

Her life sounded glamorous, but the hours were anything but. She recalled a typical day. "I would get up around six or six-thirty A.M. and run five or six miles, rain or shine, sleet or snow. Then I would get into my full regalia of a suit and heels and start making calls for the events and answering e-mails. At six P.M. or so, I would head out to two, three, or four events until about ten P.M. each night. Then I'd go home to answer more e-mails, prepare another proposal, get a press kit together, work on my newsletter, and then go to bed between midnight and two A.M. That was six days a week. Sunday, I'd crash."

Courtney's daily routine is an example of the way good girls start out, especially at jobs they love. While this kind of regimen can be maintained in doses, it's difficult to keep up this pace without suffering some side effects of stress like headaches, neckaches, even depression.

Courtney loved her work and bit by bit let it become the sum of her late-twenties existence. Like other good girls, her life narrowed to include only her job, and the simple pleasures of life slipped away. "I'd read those stories in Wired magazine where they asked, 'What book are you reading now?' and I was surprised to realize that I never read a book that whole time. I was so busy just trying to keep up with the daily running of my business. When people would ask, 'What do you do for fun?' I would wonder, 'Sleep?' Everything during that time was really all about my work. Yes, there were parties and sure there were moments when I was having fun, but it really was my job."

Her enthusiasm was contagious, and her parents were proud that their daughter was on a fast track so quickly. She was almost famous, with her party press appearing in The New Yorker and Harper's Bazaar. With her intense schedule, she was only able to spend real time with family on holidays, but her dad lived close by and actually pitched in to help her business. "Bless his heart, he came to every single one of my New York cocktail parties," she said. "He helped me set up. He was bartender. He helped me with coat check. He was really wonderful. I could see that he wanted me to succeed, but it was especially nice because I was always trying to make my parents proud of me."

Her parents' approval served as both the recognition for her success and the motivation to do more. "Nicole Kidman, during her Oscar acceptance speech said something like, 'I just wanted to say I'm so glad that I can finally please my mother.' And I thought, She's an Oscar-winning actress and she's still worried about her mother's approval! And yet that's how I felt, too."

Courtney had a team of people working for her, but the work fell largely on her shoulders, by choice. It's not unusual for overachieving women to try to do it all themselves, since, after all, who could do a better job? Courtney believed, "I didn't have someone to whom I could say, 'Just go to that party for me and write it up!' They'd never get it back to me the right way, or people would say that they wanted to see Courtney."

Courtney rationalized that the success was worth the stress and the busyness. "It was really, really insanely busy, but it also was very energizing as much as it was exhausting because I fed off the energy of other people. The frenetic pace that everyone was experiencing really kept me going."

She bought into the "everybody's busy" gospel. She likened her endurance and her adrenaline rush to the experience of running a marathon. "Even if you're at the twenty-sixth mile and you hit the wall, you still have two rows of people cheering you on. Like running a race, even if my body isn't in it anymore, I'm just being pushed by the momentum. So I just keep going." Courtney kept running until she hit a financial wall.

Her business slowed down with the economy just as the pressure from her peers and her colleagues kicked up. Her continued desire to appease all her constituencies made the tension worse. "From the end of 2000 through the beginning of 2001, I could see that things were starting to get more difficult. I just had so much going on and people had expectations of me. Everyone always wanted to know what my exit strategy was and when we were going public." Even her employees tightened the screws. "I was starting to have pressure from my employees, who were pulling on me, saying, 'We want stock options.' Everybody was getting a little inflated and wanting more and more for less and less."

Each month that passed, business got worse. "When the market crashed, things started falling apart." Her revenue model depended on corporate marketing budgets that were being cut. Clients started to delay their commitments, but Courtney's own costs kept mounting. "It was getting tougher and tougher. No one was spending money."

Then 9/11 happened. She had to let people go. "I was trying to manage everything on my own again, with all these other demands and stresses of just being a single businessperson in New York. I realized I had to start figuring out what to do, which was terrifying."

Courtney is an extremely quick-thinking and talented woman. But, because she was in such a stressed situation, she couldn't see her way out of her mess. This is where the quiet space and perspective of a little time off can uncloud some of the catastrophic thoughts that paralyze action. But Courtney took another course.

"I did the worst thing," she said. "I decided to get married. It was all so fast. We met in January of 2002. He proposed in April. He pursued me very aggressively and swept me off my feet, which was easy to do because I was in this vulnerable point with my career. He promised to take care of me in California while I worked on rebuilding my business. So I thought, Okay, I can just start again."

What Courtney really did was run away from her problems. "I switched my focus from 'what am I doing with my career?' to being engaged," she admitted. "I just wanted to believe in the future. I had my doubts, but he was so confident that he kind of carried me along. We got married in August. It was a disaster from the third day of the honeymoon. I left in September. The fairy tale collapsed and I scrambled back to New York."

Without money or a job and her new marriage in ruins, Courtney said, "It was my own personal ground zero. I had to declare bank-ruptcy. I was trying to figure out, 'Do I file for divorce in New York or California?' The whole year was just off the charts. I felt like all I could do was curl up in a ball and sleep. I definitely knew that I needed to give myself a nice long amount of time off. I knew I couldn't say, 'I'm taking a few weeks' or 'I'm taking a month.' I just said, 'I'm taking a year.' And I did."

At first Courtney escaped into being alone. "I spent the winter reading the classics and books about female rage and anger. I allowed myself to have those feelings. I also got a puppy, which really turned my perspective." Eventually she got a job as an office manager to support herself, though the tasks of organizing a small office were much less harrowing than her former existence.

"As soon as I got a job, my parents were relieved, because I was getting myself back on my feet. They thought I took too long with my emotional time-out. I thought I'd just wallow in it until I wallowed out of it."

Thanks to her time off, Courtney is now approaching her next career with open eyes. "It took me a full year and I'm just now get-ting to feel like the wheels of inspiration are beginning to start to creak forward again. I learned that I don't have to be the number one star. Part of my time-off learning is that I just cannot muster the energy to get the 'public Courtney' out there when internally I'm exhausted. That's one of my biggest discoveries and the thing that I'm working on—doing what Courtney really wants, not just what the 'Courtney-people-think-they-know' wants.

"A life means so many more things than what's in your bank account or how well known you are. Money really doesn't buy hap-piness. Having the fanciest life and being famous isn't important to me anymore. I am beginning to understand what I really want, but taking time to let it solidify and still searching on the path to get me there. Whatever I do, I'll be happy doing it. I know I can move on."

Imagine what a classified advertisement for your current work situation would be. Would you answer the ad for YOUR own life?

WANTED: Perpetually peppy person needed for well-paid, senior-level management position. Must be willing to sacrifice a personal life, contact with friends and family, and all hopes of serenity. Eagerness to overdeliver a plus and a high tolerance for stress mandatory. Compensation is competitive, but will never be enough.

Now, fill it in for yourself and the job you do.

WANTED: _____

_____

_____

_____

_____

If you wouldn't answer the ad, why not? _____

_____

Who should? _____

_____

What would be your ideal job description? _____

_____

_____

Would you take a pay cut to get the job? _____

_____

What would you give up to get it? _____

_____

Time Off for Good Behavior

Would it require changes in your nonwork life? _____

_____

_____

_____

Type As like to get their way and they are often impatient for results. Write down your five most stubborn habits:

1. _____
2. _____
3. _____
4. _____
5. _____

If there are a few you'd like to break, could you prescribe an antidote?_____

_____

_____

Do you bore easily? _____

Could you force yourself to do one thing at a time for 24 hours?

_____

If not, why not? _____

_____

Good girls like to support everyone else's needs. Whose needs are you supporting? _____

_____

_____

Which ones can you let go of? _____

_____

CHAPTER FOUR

Your Money or Your Life?

What's the one thing that stands between a burned-out good girl and time off? Many of us would answer money. Beyond ego, beyond the fear of others' reactions, lurks the practical consideration of how to afford to take some time when we still have to make a living.

Money is not only the way we pay bills and protect our future. As Type A good girls, we believe that money is the marker of achievement. It's a measure of how hard we work, how much we've grown in our careers. It's the lure that makes us work harder and it's the handcuff that keeps us at the job. It's also an excuse to avoid the challenge of re-creating our lives. Getting money under our control with a solid financial plan is the key to the ability to take time off when we need it.

What Money Means to Good Girls

In the early years, raises are a form of approval and recognition. As our obligations expand to include our families, our children, and our parents' care, money is the tool to sustain and nurture them. As our careers move on, money is competitive currency:

"How much better am I doing than my peers?" And at some point, money becomes the only life raft we're holding on to when our jobs fail to satisfy us. "At least I'm making a lot of money."

Money is why so many women will persist in difficult circumstances. Even as hard-charging accomplished women, we fear that we won't be able to get another job or that without that same amount of money everything that we've worked for will fall apart. So we don't leave. But sticking it out and ignoring the stress can backfire and result in behaviors that get us fired anyway.

This chapter will lay out the money issues a step at a time.

Count Up Your Vacation

First of all, we don't have to abandon our jobs entirely to get time off. If you've got the "worn-out" feeling that cries for weeks of escape, take a deep breath and get real. While you might want to fly around the world or curl into a child's pose in a yoga retreat for a year, think about what really makes sense for your life.

To me, five weeks seemed like a lifetime, since I had gone so long without taking meaningful time off, yet it's a laughable length of time by academic sabbatical standards, and it's shorter than many "normal" vacations in Europe. But in the time-crazed business world, that span was a luxury. If your dream is just to take a few weeks, you don't have to quit. Check out your own vacation status first. How much time do you have coming to you? How many weekends have you worked? How many sick days are permitted, yet are still untaken? Many companies also offer a couple of discretionary personal days.

Total those days and see if they're enough for the rest you need. Though company policy may officially discourage more than two weeks in a row or disallow the use of untaken sick days as vacation days, you need to impress upon your boss the importance of making an exception in this case.

If you're one of the millions of women who never takes the vacation you are given, the cost of your time off is zero. It's already paid for. You can take the time as your well-deserved reward.

If you're like most workers, you probably are leaving vacation days on the table. A recent survey found that "fifty-six percent of employees will be postponing their vacations until business and economic conditions improve."[1] While America may be the most productive nation, we take among the least amount of vacation days in the industrialized world. Many other countries mandate vacation. The U.S. does not.

Why does a good girl resist the idea of taking time off? Guilt may be a reason. A recent Expedia.com survey found that in America "one in five employees feels guilty taking time off."[2] Question yourself as to whether the reason you are "saving" vacation is because you're too busy to take it, or to assuage your own guilt about leaving others "abandoned." Or are you worried that you'll have to work too hard to prepare and then be overwhelmed with catching up on your return? Or perhaps you have convinced yourself that you're indispensable, even though you know that's not true.

In suggesting that you take vacation to alleviate burnout, I'm not advocating the good girl version of a vacation, aka a long weekend. While you will read of some women who told me they got back on track after a week off, most of us need more time than that to clear the fog out of our minds. A book called *Take Back Your Time: Fighting Overwork and Time Poverty in America,* notes the phenomenon of "vacation deficit disorder" coined by Anders Hayden.[3] Chapter author Joe Robinson cites a study by the University of Tel Aviv's Arie Shirom and S. E. Hobfoll that revealed that "one of the remarkable features of a vacation is that it helps to gather lost emotional resources crashed by burnout, such as support and a sense of mastery." The study proposed that "it takes a minimum of two full weeks for the emotional restoration process to occur."[4] That's why long weekends are not vacations. You need time to fully unwind and restore your body and mind.

If your untaken time is significant enough for your time-off needs, then your only challenge is convincing your company that you can take it all at once. Be prepared to think through how your responsibilities can be covered in your absence. If you hope to return, that's your job to figure out, not theirs.

Be honest about the workload on your plate, as well as the cycles of activity within your business. Accountants can't stomp out on April 1st and expect a welcome mat for their return. Retailers can't retreat when the holiday season is at full tilt. Think forward, as if you were your boss, and consider when would be the best time for the company, not just for yourself. That will help you craft a winning pitch. However, be careful not to be overly considerate of your company's workload. We've all worked in places where no time is ideal for vacation. It's always crazy busy, something is always a bigger priority. That's a corporate culture problem, not yours to solve.

Check Out Your Company's Leave Policy

The second path is to investigate your company's policies for leaves and flexibility. Pamela Craig, senior vice president for finance for Accenture, suggests that often women aren't aware of the options that their companies offer. "They haven't had a reason to know about them, so it behooves all of us to fully explore all the options and even creatively suggest one that isn't there."

In the last chapter of the book, I'll share some of the innovative approaches that many corporations are taking to keep their best people. Some of their policies may be ones that your company already has. Also, their innovations may give you creative ideas that you can suggest to your management.

Many women assume that quitting is the only way to get away from a situation that has become unbearable or to get significant time off. That's not true, especially if you are a top performer, which as a Type A good girl, you likely are. Retaining talented women is a major focus of companies all over the country. After recruiting you, training you, and seeing the benefits of your hard work, the last thing most firms want is to see that their investment is walking out the door.

Retention is increasing as a human resources issue according to a 2004 survey conducted for the Society of Human Resource Management. In a poll of 362 executives and human resource professionals, 61 percent said they would focus more attention on employee retention, up from 51 percent last year.[5] One way of slowing down the exit is to make work respond in more flexible ways to women's needs.

Sabbaticals, fully and partly paid, benefits extensions, and reentry offers are part of recent human resource responses to this escalating need for flexible time. But not every company became enlightened on their own. Many of the programs with flexibility came about because women asked.

It Pays to Ask

Unfortunately, the first mistake most women make is to assume the worst and refuse to ask. Carnegie Mellon University Economics Professor Linda Babcock, in her book *Women Don't Ask*, traces this reluctance back to the entry moment for women in the workforce. In one study, only 7 percent of women tried to negotiate their salaries, compared to 57 percent of men, Joanne Cleaver noted in the *Chicago Tribune*, "Even seasoned women in midcareer don't try to negotiate for what they want at work—flextime, a more high-profile project, or a bigger raise."[6]

I've heard this same comment from corporate officers, who say that by the time a woman walks into her manager's office in a state of stress, she has already decided that she's leaving. She's thought it through on her own, agreed to a new plan elsewhere, and is sliding her resignation across the desk without room for discussion. And, as loyal women, once they figure out what they are going to do and make a commitment to it, their decision is already locked in. They wouldn't "go back" on the promise or arrangement once made.

That behavior is a typical good girl characteristic, feeling that only you are responsible for yourself or that you don't want to play the ultimatum game. It implies that you don't deserve special consideration, so you'll just leave rather than change the rules. Realize your value and contribution. Give your company a chance to do the right thing by you, just as you have by them. Just asking might make the issue of money moot.

If you are thinking of taking some time off, you might want to try something that doesn't involve the dramatic "stay or leave" scenario. I've had plenty of managers pull me aside to ask, "Why don't women ask or negotiate options before they quit?" One problem is that the good girls operate with absolutes. Many women, in their zeal to be 100 percent dedicated to everything they do, say, "If I can't be a hundred percent at home and a hundred percent at work, I have to leave."

Additionally, as women who prefer acceptance to conflict, we often choose to avoid a scene or the risk that negotiating might hurt a relationship, and we simply leave rather than ask. A final reason that women don't ask is that the best of the good girls don't appreciate how good they are.

You are in a strong position to negotiate. Give your company or boss the benefit of the doubt that they will want to keep you or come up with an adjusted schedule. Maybe they will, maybe they won't. But it doesn't hurt to ask.

If you are able to take a company-sponsored leave—whether it is fully paid, partially paid, or your company just continues to pay their portion of your benefits—this will take a huge weight off your mind. As you read about some of the innovative programs at the end of the book, you may be able to suggest options to your own firm.

Even if your company won't pay your salary, the other question is this: If you take the leave during their downtime, will they hold your job open, and for how long? If you still want your job but are just temporarily out of love with it, a break might give you enough time to get recharged.

To Quit or Not to Quit?

Quitting your job may feed your need for revenge and provide some immediate sense of relief, but be sure you've thought through your reasons for doing it. Unless you're independently wealthy, your grievances should be very serious, or your plan well thought out. Perhaps you have emotionally moved on to a new career path. Or you are ready to risk living off your savings until you find another job. Perhaps you have significant savings that keep you from worrying about money. Although a few of the women in this book quit on the spot, the emotional force it takes to do it and survive shouldn't be underestimated. It can be done, and it can even feel incredibly rejuvenating, but it comes with a price tag.

Quitting is a solution I'd never recommend to women who are the sole support of their families, or are barely making it paycheck to paycheck. However, I would suggest that the truly burned-out women in this category (and given their circumstances, there may be many of them) consider sitting down with friends or family members to see if there is a route to relief. Could your family take care of your children if you were to take a week to yourself? Is there anyone you can turn to for financial support, to give you the confidence to approach your company for an alternative work plan?

Sometimes the feeling of being "worn-out" can be relieved with a more flexible work arrangement. See if it's possible to put some flexibility in your life, such as a compressed work week, where you squeeze five days' work into four and get a free day. See if it's possible to learn from Xerox, which allows employees to do time shifting, so that hours can be staggered around personal needs.

Xerox observed that the employees in their customer service centers had a very high level of absenteeism. Paula Fleming, the company's director of human resource effectiveness, explained the problem. "People in call centers didn't have a lot of flexibility or control over their jobs. So when a woman would have to take a child to a doctor's appointment or go to a kid's soccer game, it was easier just to call in sick and lose the whole day. The call center statistics started going south. We found that if you create the kind of flexibility where people can come in early, leave early, or take a couple of hours off in the middle of the day for a reason, everybody's a lot happier."

In other words, taking time off during "time on" is a way to keep the wear-out under control.

The Courage to Plan

Fear of losing your job and salary can be paralyzing. We stay in the wrong jobs or postpone important personal needs while we grumble, "I can't afford to do it now." Indeed, pursuing time off takes forethought and courage. But when your peace of mind, your health, and your relationships are at stake, doing the hard planning is not so high a price to pay.

If you are honest with yourself, you might find that you don't believe that you'll ever have the sufficient resources that allow you to walk away from a job. Ann Perry, senior writer with TheStreet.com and author of *The Wise Inheritor: A Guide to Managing, Investing, and Enjoying Your Inheritance* notes that "even the most financially secure women can suffer from a pervasive fear known as 'bag-lady syndrome.' This is the deep-seated dread of running out of money in old age and having to live alone and penniless on the streets," said Ann. She's heard financial advisors who say that this fear can even affect women worth millions of dollars.

A couple of the women I interviewed raised the "bag lady" specter. Lalita had savings on her side when she left her high-level technology position. Yet, despite Lalita's careful preparations, she continued to worry about money while she was on leave. She said, "I would wake up some days and slap my head and say, 'What were you thinking? You're not earning any money. Are you nuts?' But I've always taken care of myself and if I was going to be a bag lady, then I was going to be the manager of the bag ladies, organize on the street if necessary. Something was going to work out."

It's not that women necessarily lack financial know how. They have a psychological barrier about money that may have been erected when they were young.

In research I have done about women's attitudes toward money, I've asked the question, "What was the most powerful memory of money in your life?" And so often, the answers hearkened back to their childhood. If their parents were worrisome about money, women often grew up with a fear of losing it. If their families "rated" others based on their wealth, then women harbor a secret code that equates personal value with financial worth. One financial advisor said that women still hear their parent's voice saying, "Don't quit a job till you have another one lined up." Parents raised during the Depression are particularly keen on that warning.

Those parental adages rubbed off on all of us. Allowances and bonuses were signs of Mom and Dad's approval and reward for good behavior. Ardith's dad rewarded her good grades with money. "He started a bonus system for us kids where he gave us one dollar for every A and a kicker bonus for straight As," said Ardith. Raises were worked for, too. "If you wanted a raise in your allowance, you had to stand up and make an A/V presentation on what additional chores you would do to justify your raise," she recalled, laughing.

Additionally, good girls developed their own respect and responsibility for money even as teenagers. Leslie, forty-seven, now president of a boutique recruiting firm, admits, "I was a waitress when I was fourteen, even when it was illegal. I always had a sense of responsibility for my age and I took pride in that." Lisa B., who worked three jobs at a time during college summers, said that work was just part of growing up.

Teenage good girls set financial goals and went after them. In an early display of her eventual fashion career, Joan earned a coveted dress with her own sweat. "I found a dress at Saks that I really liked. But it was one hundred and fifty dollars, and this was a long time ago. My mother said, 'Absolutely not. If you want the dress, get it yourself.' I took a job washing floors in a nursing home. I earned the money, bought the dress, and quit the job. I was very focused." She was sixteen and already had respect for the work/salary equation.

With so many years working for money, saving it and guarding against losing it, it's natural that money becomes attached to fear. The only way to alleviate the fear of not having enough money is to develop a financial plan. This isn't a simple matter of saying to yourself, Okay, I'll skip going out to dinner once a week and lay off the four-dollar lattes in the morning. If you want to have the confidence to make the right decisions about leaving or staying, meet with a financial planner and work out the numbers. How much have you saved? If you dream of a job as a bakery chef and it pays half of your salary as an art director, is that numerically realistic? What will you have to make in order to maintain the lifestyle you need?

If you read this and your eyes start to glaze over as you begin, dreading the chore of figuring out your personal finances, you're not alone. Ann Perry acknowledges that "successful career women, especially those overseeing numbers of employees and making big incomes, sometimes find it difficult to realize a basic money truth: making it and managing it are two different things."

There are issues you will need to face if you decide that quitting is the only answer. Your benefits don't go with you if you leave, but COBRA helps you bridge the gap for up to eighteen months. However, there are other steps you ought to consider. Ann advises, "It's critical that you maintain health, life, and disability insurance (if you plan to continue working)—and that you have an emergency fund that will cover expenses for three to six months, if possible." (Think of this as the answer to the ghoulish question, "What if you get hit by a truck just after you quit?")

Ann contends that "your backup emergency fund should be a home-equity line of credit on your home, if you own one. Note that this line of credit must be secured while you still have your job, since you need to be employed in order to get one. If you walk into the bank to apply for it one day after you quit, you'll be out of luck. Remember, too, that if you've got a loan outstanding from your 401(k) plan when you leave, the IRS considers it an early withdrawal that will cost you roughly half of what you borrowed in taxes and penalties, when you might least be able to afford it."

The best way to avoid these last-minute concerns is to develop a financial plan with an advisor and update it every year. "I recommend seeking help from a professional on this," said Ann. "Most of us wouldn't dream of making major repairs on our cars or computers ourselves, but somehow feel we can plan something as important and complex as financial security for the rest of our lives without assistance." She notes that a small but growing number of financial planners also offer coaching or "life planning" along with financial advice, which might be just what you need when you are contemplating change. Once you're not panicked over whether you can make ends meet, you can approach the issue of time off with more comfort.

Suzette Gross, employee relations manager with American Express, says that her tendency to be a long-term planner has made all the difference. "I always have a backup plan. I always think very clearly about what's my plan B, what's my plan C, what if? Because I think that in the long run that really reduces stress and if something happens, I'm not scrambling. And that goes with every activity—childcare, job planning, finances."

Making a plan takes work. But it can give you the freedom to choose and the control of your choices if you need time off. Before you say, "I can't," listen to these women who learned that they could. They saved, they planned, they turned getting fired or getting hurt into getting free. A few did it the hard way. But these examples show there's more than one way to get time off.

Working Hard for the Money

I'll start with my own financial situation. Like many good girls, I had a few weeks of untaken vacation so my leave was practically a free ride. But if I had had to quit to get the time, I was financially prepared to sustain our life for a good while without my salary.

We had a financial plan, but even with that, my childhood money triggers kicked in. Joe and I had never raised our style of living at the same pace as our income, yet I never felt complacent about money. With my modest upbringing, no matter how much money I made and saved, I couldn't let go of the responsibility to bring home the bacon.

Money was my reward for giving up so much of my life. My salary was my good girl way of keeping score, trading As for dollar signs, blue ribbons for raises. I understand the fears of losing it. That's why I approached my boss to seek a way to get the time without losing my job.

Rosemary looked at her earnings and savings from her years running the childcare company she founded as an investment that she could cash in. When she decided to resign, she said, "I see taking this time off as a return on my investment [ROI] for the last eleven years. I am proud to have the courage to take it, not to choose something else quickly or out of fear."

Eleven years of giving yourself to a job should add up to some ROI. We wait for retirement at sixty-five or seventy as the first chance to reap the rewards of our hard work. Many women have learned that it's not necessary to wait that long to enjoy a break. And, in fact, your life may not give you that chance anyway.

Risk/Reward

Among the women I interviewed, each woman took her own level of financial risk. Liz had the same attitude toward saving over the years as I did. She had a proactive financial plan from the start of her career. "Because I had been conscious in my thirties that I wanted to do something very different in my forties, I had saved a lot of money. I didn't have to worry financially if it took me two or three years to figure out something that would actually pay me. I knew I wouldn't starve and that meant a lot to me."

But Liz had this to say to women who aren't in her position. "I remember sitting in my bedroom in Portland, saying, 'I've got the money in the bank, I have no dependents. If I can't do this, who can?' I really admire the people that can make the leap I made, but without the financial safety net that I had."

Remembering that Liz was walking away from a truly exciting job, running women's marketing for Nike, I'm not sure everyone would agree that her move was without risk.

Getting an A in Organization

Jane C., forty-six, a teacher of special needs high schoolers in Pennsylvania, had her daughter Kate when she was thirty-six and she took nine months' maternity leave. "That was nice," Jane said, "but a monkey could have been there and she wouldn't really know the difference. I wanted to be around for her first school experience. So I planned from birth that I was going to stay home with her when she was four."

Jane approached her school personnel director who explained what she needed to do to make that happen. "To justify the sabbatical, I needed to take nine college credits a semester while I was off. And I put money away every paycheck for four years."

Jane also admitted that one way she compensated for her reduced income was to sign up for an extra credit card in her name. She used it to charge some of the things that she needed for her time with Kate and for family expenses and then paid it off slowly as she returned to work. Though she's not someone who generally relies on credit for what she can't afford, she found that the risk (and avoiding asking her husband for every small thing) was worth the peace of mind she had for that year.

Some women sought expert help. After Julie decided that her situation in her Washington, D.C., consulting firm had become untenable, she resigned, but she gave two months notice so they—and she—could plan. "I had time to get my arrangements in order and pack my house up," she said, and she met with a financial advisor to work out specifics for her time away. Her goal was to take a year to travel and she was set on not exceeding her means.

Tied to the issue of losing your salary if you quit or take an unpaid leave without a job guarantee is the worry that you won't find an equal position. But Julie was so ready for a break, she assumed that even if the worst happened, she'd find a job.

"I knew that I had talents and skills and that I would find something once I got back," she said. "It's nice to be the one in charge, but if I have to flip burgers, that's okay, too. I knew that I could rely on myself to find work and to feed and clothe myself, regardless of what I had to do."

Take the Money and Run

In the last few years, it's become common for companies to reduce their costs and workforce by offering early retirement or voluntary separation packages to those who leave. Even with that lifeline, some women don't take advantage because they are uncertain about whether they are ready to be on their own or look for something new. Others take the money, but quickly seek out a replacement job without giving themselves the time to consider what they really want to do next.

You might not greet an offer to leave with open arms. Your ego might be bruised. You might feel that desperate need to run to another job for assurance that your career isn't over. Or you might pause and look at your offer as an opportunity to get the time you wanted (and it's paid!).

A friend of mine was offered the choice to either separate from her merging corporation or stick it out through the transition, and that's when it all clicked for her. "The door opened and I had to choose. Either I could kick it open or I could put a barricade in front of it and grind it out." She kicked the door open and left.

Both Bonnie and Diane had just hit their fifties when they were offered generous packages. Even though both loved their jobs, they decided to use the chance to take some time and to design new careers of their own.

When Donna D. was forty-one and grieving from her husband's death, her company happened to announce an opportunity for long service people to take a voluntary separation package. "They were trying to get people who were close to retirement, but due to my tenure with the company and my age, I was able to ask for it," she said. "It turned out to be a real gift for my life."

Being offered the money to go might seem like a dream situation, but I've heard women say that they are still reluctant to let go, even when the money is handed to them. Type A ego may be one of the reasons.

Loss of future earning potential is also a potent lure to stay. Ardith realized that money had kept her in place even when she wanted to leave. "One of the hardest things about leaving is that there was always an incentive or stock options in the future. It's hard to walk away, even if you have enough money."

Quit or Bust

Type A good girls aren't quitters. And they generally don't make rash moves, especially where financial and emotional security is concerned. But a few women were so weary and angry that they walked out the door with no plan. When she was thirty-three, Cindy quit her consulting firm at lunchtime, and took three months off. "The three months were actually calculated based on how much money I had in my bank account. That's when I would have to start earning money again."

Kerry, who took several short leaves in her twenties, took a more cavalier view of the money issue. "I felt, I'm young, I've got money. It wasn't like I was not going to get another job. The only thing I had to worry about was rent, and even so, I sublet my apartment when I decided to go overseas. It was easy to do. I didn't have any children, I wasn't married, I wasn't supporting anyone. I had COBRA. Why not do it?"

Not everyone is confident (or foolhardy) enough to live freestyle without a financial plan. The resultant stress may not be worth the price. At the start of her leave, Lisa B. remembers, "I was in a tail-spin, wanting to quickly replace my job with something, because it was like a drug. I didn't leave with pay. I was going right into my nest egg."

Lisa B.'s philosophy about taking the leap without a plan was this. "My panic was self-created, because I had plenty of money to live on. You'd be surprised how little you really need when you have time to do your own ironing, watch your own dog, do your own grocery shopping, and not eat fast food five nights a week."

Still, Lisa pieced together consulting and sales jobs to restore the income she needed to move her life forward. However, there's no substitute for a serious financial plan that's thought through in advance.

What's Really Keeping You?

While the fear of losing money is the excuse for not leaving, it's not the only reason women stick it out. The fear of the unknown also pins us to our seats. What will I do afterward? What will people think? Where will I be day to day without my job, my office to go to, and my work friends to talk to? What am I really meant to do with my life?

Dr. Kaye Moore describes the unknown as a fear of floating. "Right now you have structure. You may feel that if the structure goes out from under you, you're going to be out there floating in kind of an abyss. That's a huge psychological barrier that is very difficult for women to confront. The irony is that, when you make a change, there is a sense of well-being that you never could have imagined before."

Lydia Mallet, vice president and chief diversity officer of General Mills, agrees. "The risk you perceive is never as great as you think it is. If you can follow your informed instinct, it will serve you well."

Getting informed about your finances is critical to giving yourself the confidence and independence to manage the ups and downs of your career. Questions at the end of this chapter will help you get your thinking started if you don't already have a financial plan.

But most important is finding a financial planner. Where to start? First, ask your friends and family for recommendations of people they trust. Referrals can also be obtained through National Planning Association, the membership organization of certified financial planners, at www.fpanet.org and the National Association of Personal Financial Advisors, an organization of fee-only advisors, at www.napfa.org. Look for planners who work with clients like you. Arrange to meet with at least three of them (most charge nothing for a one-hour introductory session) and find one with the right personal chemistry.

Additional financial advice and planning is just a mouse click away. In a November 2000 article, *Time* columnist Sharon Epperson, who is CNBC's personal finance correspondent, reviews some of the more worthy financial websites for women, including www.wfn.com and www.msmoney.com.[7] Add to them general planning sites like www.SmartMoney.com, www.Money.com, www.Kiplinger.com, www.wsj.com, and www.CNBC.com on MSN. SmartMoney.com worksheets to help you calculate where you stand and how you spend are included at the end of this chapter.

Once you know where you stand, you can figure out what you'll need to do to feel financially confident about taking some time. How long to take depends on a combination of factors: your family/financial situation, how tired or burned out you are, how much you are willing to dip into your savings, if necessary, what dreams you hope to pursue (and the price of those dreams), and your knowledge of yourself. In other words, how much time will it take to get you back on track?

In my case, I originally underestimated how much time to take, thinking, Oh, if I take three weeks off, I'll be a new person. A wise friend told me, "Mary Lou, you will blow through that time and not even get to the point of thinking clearly . . . take at least six weeks to feel the effect." I chickened out and made it five, but in retrospect, I wish I had taken six months. One guarantee: No matter how long your leave, you will never wish you'd taken less time.

Also, as you consider the potential lost income and start to worry about how long it may take to replace your job if you leave for good, remember this: The skills that got you to where you are are yours for the taking. Your track record, your talents, and your network of contacts and clients will be there for you on "the other side." You are not a woman without resources. Your tenacious Type A good girl style will help you find your next passion.

Making a Life-changing Financial Choice: Ardith's Story

Although I have known Ardith for twelve years, I had no idea that she and her partner Dave dreamed of retirement at fifty. The two of them worked hard and saved carefully until unexpected news shook up their well-laid plans. When Ardith was forty, the company she worked for was bought by a larger one, and her hold on her high-level job was precarious. Consolidations were being discussed.

As a marketing officer, Ardith worked the long and grueling hours familiar to anyone in a high-pressure industry. "For years, I was living in New York and commuting to Connecticut. I'd get up very early and I'd skip breakfast to catch the train. I didn't read the paper because I was always preparing for my first meeting at eight-thirty. At lunch, I'd just grab a sandwich to eat at my desk and wouldn't leave work till six-thirty or seven, only because that's when the last shuttle left for the train." By evening, she and her husband were too tired to do anything but order takeout six nights a week, which, as she admitted, "wasn't all that healthy." She would watch an hour of TV, fall asleep exhausted, and wake up and do it all over again.

Ardith and Dave had talked for years about the idea of retiring to some idyllic location in their fifties. That's when they'd have saved enough to afford a lifestyle that was a little less dependent on full-time work. No matter how much she'd dreamed of someday leaving, the lure of future rewards and the need to save for her long-term plan kept her in her chair. As she got promoted again and again, "There was always promised money that I couldn't walk away from, like incentive or stock options."

When her company was taken over, it was a defining moment. The bad news of losing her job was balanced by the good news of her package. "At the takeover, everything was vested. I could take all the money and I was getting fired anyway. I was out of a job and there wasn't anything holding me."

This sounded ideal, except that Ardith's hard-working habits kicked in. Her first instincts were to replace her job with something else. "I started getting a visceral gut reaction that I ought to prepare to interview in the tri-state area. But I was tired, and a little burned-out."

Ardith started to question her own motivations for the first time. "I didn't feel that my ego was tied to becoming CEO or chief market-ing officer. I had to ask myself, Why am I denying myself the chance to do other things, just so I can keep being VP? I had to ask, Why am I doing this? I had the chance to do things that I had more passion for. What do I want to do versus what have I always done?"

As Ardith considered her own decision, she realized that Dave was a kind of role model for her. "He had quit his corporate job and was already a consultant with flexibility. Since Dave stepped off the track, I could see that someone could get out of corporate life and still feed themselves."

Ardith went back to the plans she had made for her dream escape. She'd actually written up a weekly schedule of events for how she hoped she'd live her life.

Ardith's story reminded me of my own amnesia. When I finally left my CEO job, I found two earlier lists I had written that described the way I wanted to live my life. Somehow those lists got ignored while the daily "to-do" rundowns were constantly studied and expanded. Like me, Ardith needed to face the truth of what she'd written.

She and her husband thought about the choice. Should she save the severance and keep working in another corporate job for another ten years, or should they make the move? "We asked ourselves, How much money do we need?"

Ardith applied her Type A organizational skills to her potential time-off life. "We made a list of criteria: low humidity, the best weather possible, arts and culture, golf and tennis, interesting people, and better value for our money. Santa Fe, Boulder, and Napa made the cut. We took a six-day trip, two days in each place, back to back. We met with realtors, interviewed friends who lived there, and hung out in the downtown area at night. We liked the total vibe of Santa Fe. It's stunningly beautiful. People who come here are entrepreneurial like us."

Ardith and Dave packed up their lives and relocated to Santa Fe. Her move surprised many of her friends because her good behavior gave no indication that she'd be the "kind" of woman to do just what she wanted to do. "I learned that people had a perception of me that I never had. 'You'll be back in six months,' they said."

Her day-to-day life is close to the dream list that she had imagined for years. "I wanted to exercise, ski, go to classes, learn Italian, travel more, own a dog, entertain people once a month, go to movies once a week, do community things, such as my committee work at the Georgia O'Keeffe Museum, and volunteer at an animal shelter. And I do marketing projects, two days a week at the most, since we hadn't totally hit our goal number."

She has learned that part-time work suits her. "I realize now there are jobs that require fewer hours in the day and yet still provide you with enough money to sustain yourself. I don't have paid health benefits, but I can make this work."

Except for the perks, Ardith says she doesn't miss her job anymore. "I definitely like not having to wear a suit. I've barely thought about Connecticut, New York, or the company. I'm still in the honeymoon phase. I liked a lot of parts of my job, but there were also frustrations. Now it's just me."

Ardith respects the good fortune of her situation. "This is a decision of privilege, to be able to opt out or downshift. I lucked out a lot on the stock options through no skill or work of my own." (Ardith shows her good girl tendencies here, as if her hard work had nothing to do with her earned rewards.)

Despite her good fortune, Ardith acknowledges the difficulty of walking away from what's familiar. "It takes courage to step out of the comfort track that you're in and start cross-country skiing where there aren't any track marks. There are a lot of people who could, but don't."

Ardith's decision may have seemed easy, but she's still concerned about the availability of part-time assignments and, since she's only forty-three, she still has many years to sustain this ideal life. But she's finally realized why she made the right decision. "I wasn't escaping, I was going toward something that I wanted more. My work isn't my life."

FINANCIAL HEALTH CHECK

You might have been too busy before to give much thought to where your money goes and how it grows. But at this important juncture in your life, you need to know your net worth, how much you are spending (if money is going to be tight), and whether you're adequately protecting yourself and your assets. While you ought to consult with a financial planner, these worksheets will give you a quick review of what you need to know about your money.

The following charts and directions are reprinted with permission from www.smartmoney.com. If you click on their website, you can actually use the online calculator to work up your numbers.

How Much Are You Worth?

Www.SmartMoney.com asks, "Where do you stand financially? When you get done with this net worth worksheet, you may be surprised at how much you own. The idea here is to total up all your assets (house, car, retirement plan) and subtract your liabilities (credit card debt, mortgage). The result can be used as a baseline as you think about planning for the future. Remember, however, this calculator doesn't account for any taxes owed on proceeds in an investment portfolio or retirement account."

ASSETS		DEBTS	
Checking account		Mortgage	
Savings account		Personal loans	
Money-market account		Home-equity loan	
Certificates of deposit		Car loan	
Mutual funds		Other installment loans	
U.S. Treasury bills		Life insurance loans	
Stocks		Loans against investments	
Bonds		Student loans	
Cash value of life insurance policy		Credit card debts	
Trust funds			
Company savings accounts			
Cash value of pension			
Stock options			
Equity value of business			
401(k)			
IRA or KEOGH			
Other investments			
Money owed you			
Value of home			
Value of car		Total Assets	
Furnishings		Total Debts	
Collectibles		NET WORTH	
Jewelry			
Other luxury goods			

As you fill in the net worth chart and assess your results, Ann Perry suggests that you:

- Review your net worth once a year when you do your taxes.
- Strive to make your worth grow each year, through increased savings and investments in your retirement plans.
- During the annual review, take time to write down what you want

to achieve with your career and net worth in one year, five years, and ten years.

Your next step is to look at your cash flow. If you plan to live on less for a while or dip into your savings, you need to know how much money you require each month. Start by tracking where every dollar goes for one month. This will help you set priorities and break bad habits. Maybe some of your monthly expenses—forty dollars for your nails, two hundred dollars on lunches out, and twenty dollars in late video rental fees—are keeping you from reaching your goals, and, in fact, might be reduced if you take a leave that allows a more relaxed style of day-to-day living.

What's Your Cash Flow?

On their Web site, www.SmartMoney.com asks, "When it comes right down to it, do you really have any idea how much you spend each month? Do you know what's left over? Until you can answer those questions, it will be difficult to assess how much you have to invest. This worksheet asks you for estimates of typical monthly and annual expenses and subtracts them from your income to calculate your personal bottom line. If you have a recent pay stub, your checkbook, and a recent bank statement (so you don't forget those automatic withdrawals), you should be all set to go."

MONTHLY EXPENSES

Mortgage/rent	
Credit card payments	
Other debt	
Utilities	
Cable	
Internet Service	
Garbage removal	
Telephone	
Newspaper delivery	
Bank charges	
Childcare	
Clothing	
Grooming	
Entertainment (movies, arts, dining)	
Life insurance	
Disability insurance	
Health insurance	
Car payment	
Car insurance	
Commuting	
Dry cleaning	
Groceries	
Health club	
Other	
Subtotal	

ANNUAL EXPENSES

Retirement account deposits	
Deposits to investments	
Magazine subscriptions	
Current tuition	
Children's extracurricular activities	
Medical expenses	
Membership dues	
Sports/hobbies	
Travel	
Other	
Subtotal	

ANNUAL INCOME

Net salary	
Weekly	
Investment income	
Interest on bank accounts	
Bonus	
Other	
Subtotal	

Monthly Income	
Monthly Spending	

In addition to your current expenses, you ought to consider what will happen if you leave your job and the effect it will have on your cash. Ann Perry says, "It is imperative that you have health insurance. By law, many employees can continue coverage for eighteen months under their former employer, but at a higher cost. Check with an insurance broker to learn if a better alternative is available."

She adds that life insurance is another consideration. "If you had life insurance through your employer's group plan, there's a good chance you could find a less-expensive policy on your own. You need life insurance if someone relies on you for financial support. Should you plan to start another job, don't forget disability insurance. This protects your most valuable asset, your ability to earn. And during what might be a stressful time, be sure to maintain adequate insurance on home, cars, and other valuables. Coordinate these with umbrella insurance, which is relatively expensive and protects against unlikely but potentially ruinous civil liability suits."

CHAPTER FIVE

The Moment of Truth

No matter how much you try to control your circumstances, life happens. You may get an unwelcome wake-up call. A big birthday arrives or a small lump appears. A sick child needs special attention or a loved one dies. Your company is taken over. You run out of steam. For many good girls, the A-ha moment comes as the shock that makes them face their addiction to overwork. And not soon enough.

Women have asked me, "When was the moment you knew you had to quit?" I suppose we are all watching for that giant billboard that announces, "Career pothole ahead!" or "Look out, drop off into abyss of exhaustion ... NEXT!"

Maybe we want to be reassured that we don't have to worry ... yet. We're not *that* bad, so we can keep on swimming, even when the current gets rough. But sometimes the waves of overwork just inch up, washing over us before we even know we're drowning.

No matter how severe or subtle their situation, the women I interviewed used a lot of emotional language to describe the sudden realization of the crisis in their everyday lives: "I hit the wall." "I woke up." "I snapped to." "It hit me right between the eyes." The images are violent and cathartic and scary.

One woman shared with me the most painful description of a life out of control: "I was screaming inside." Imagine the stressful effects on a woman who's smiling while screaming inside. Good girls don't give up easily. After all those years of being the "go-to" women, they are not about to be labeled as quitters.

I think back to my own early report cards and that A in perseverance. Sticking it out, no matter what—that's what I was known for. Even when my ad agency hit some really low lows, I never considered leaving. Why? I refused to abandon my team. I assumed I could fix the problems with a little more time. I didn't want to be perceived as a wimp who couldn't take the heat. I didn't want to disappoint my family. I didn't want to lose. I had more than enough reasons to keep losing sleep, rather than face the reality that I was tired out from trying.

At some point in every hardworking woman's life, we face a moment of truth when we look at our lives and our work and ask, "Is this what I was meant to do?" Lurking behind that question is its nagging corollary, "How can I get some time to figure that question out?"

Moments of truth arrive without an appointment. Some of these good girls were fired, with no time to plan. Others got seriously ill or the death of a friend or family member awakened them to their own mortality. All of a sudden, the "important meetings" and "critical deadlines" pale by comparison.

Stress Is Not a Contest

I will share some dramatic stories to show how far women will persist before raising the white flag, but with this caution: You don't have to be "queen for a day" to deserve some time off.

Queen for a Day was a popular sixties game show, sort of a precursor to today's reality shows. To get on the show, women submitted their really sad stories. Maybe they had a dozen kids with no shoes, or were losing their homes, and/or they had a horrible, debilitating disease. The woman with the worst story won and her story would reduce the audience to tears. As compensation, the "queen" would win a suite of Broyhill furniture or a combination washer and dryer. She would weep with joy as she sat on a faux throne with a crown on her head.

Don't wait for the bigger-than-life crisis. Falling out of love with your life is reason enough to stop to take stock of where you are. That said, some of the life-and-death stories that follow may make you feel that your own situation isn't bad enough. On the other hand, you might start to feel that yours is worse. Many women have a tendency to out-martyr each other, sort of a "my pain is worse than yours" competition.

You may feel that some of these women give in to burnout too easily. "Big deal, she was only thirty." Or, "She worked hard, she had a great job and a terrific guy, so what if she was tired. Get over it!" None of us can live another's life and truly know how exhausted she feels.

Perhaps you will see scraps of your own life or pieces of women you know. And in seeing the symptoms, you might attempt an intervention . . . or even grab a life preserver yourself.

Life and Death

I worked with Jane B., a human resources professional, in the nineties. As long as I've known her, Jane has been "chipper." That was her good girl persona. "When I hit thirty-five," she said, "I hit a wall. I didn't have much going on socially and I thought, If I'm ever going to have a baby and get off this track, I need to leave New York."

She left for a job in Boston, and ended up working even more challenging hours. While there, Jane got seriously ill and eventually returned to New York. We worked together for several years, many of them in a state of business crisis, but Jane stayed pretty even-keeled.

"On August 1 of 2001, I lost my job," she said. "One week later, my thirty-seven-year-old brother dropped dead. Then, a month later, September 11th happened. I was reeling. I took four months to decide what to do. When the world blew up in September, I thought, I'm going to do it now if I'm ever going to do it." Jane used this grieving time to start to rethink her priorities.

September 11th emerged in several interviews as the horrific catalyst for self-evaluation. Although Kerry ultimately quit her intense public relations job because she was unhappy, 9/11 was the real turning point. Just thirty, Kerry had already taken a couple of short time offs between jobs, and they "helped me run the last couple of miles, but I wasn't learning anymore. I didn't want to manage people anymore. I felt like my office was a cage." Kerry worked near the World Trade Center. "I ran upstairs to our deck and saw the two buildings fall down. I gave notice soon after."

Like Kerry, Julie was already frustrated with her government consulting job when September 11th made her stop in her tracks. "I really wanted to experience life to the fullest. When I was eighty, I didn't want my stories of my life to be about when the copier broke down."

When death comes closer to home, the inevitable questions appear. "The turning point event for me was my mother dying," said Debra. "Somebody said to me, 'In order for you to be as old for your kids as your mother was for you, you have to live another forty years, and I just don't know if you're going to make it that long with the track you're on.'" She went to Florida for her mother's memorial service. "There were one hundred people there, and each one of them had something to say about how she had touched them. I realized that the measure of your life isn't about whether you had a big title or made a lot of money."

There's nothing like death to wake us up to having a perspective on life. A friend of mine told me that her A-ha moment came when she was almost hit by a bus on her way to work. Once at her desk, she stopped in shock, wondering, What would they write on my tombstone if I died today? She took three months off to change her epitaph.

Cindy's A-ha moment came after a close friend died from AIDS.

"I had this particularly challenging year. I was stressed-out from travel. I felt like I had little control over things, how often I traveled, how long I was away." While she was away, her friend died and a memorial service was planned. The service was a week away when Cindy made a crucial decision.

"I was thinking about getting ready for two work deadlines, with projects due the day after the service. I had this image of myself going through a very hectic, stressful day, when I would probably not eat, go down to the memorial service, and blurt out some eulogy that I hadn't given much thought to, get back in a cab, and work all night and just drop exhausted the next day. I thought, No, that's not the way I am going to remember my friend."

Cindy went out to the beach to think, and her moment of decision came at the edge of a cliff. "I thought, Just jump without knowing where you're going to land! I wasn't going to take my life. I knew I didn't have to worry about figuring everything out. Just once, I thought, Cut loose without knowing what your next step is going to be. I went back to the city and quit. I did the eulogy just the way I thought it should be done. It was the hardest thing I ever did. But everything about it felt right."

Health Check

Serious health issues can also force a change. Donna D. told her story: "My first marriage was to Michael, who was diagnosed with leukemia a month before we married. He went into remission, and they told us we couldn't have any kids. But we ended up getting pregnant with my son, David, and then the baby got cancer. I had to have his left eye removed. You just look at your life, and you think, Gosh, if I can get through this, I can get through anything."

Given her personal situation, she recalled her bosses worrying, "We can't promote her, she won't be able to handle it." In defiance of the odds, Donna was promoted and transferred to Cincinnati.

But even as she set to work again, her sadness escalated and she realized that she had to take a break to reconfigure her life. "I started realizing that I had been on this treadmill for so long. I stepped back and took time off."

Lisa K. was twenty-eight and working serious overtime at a consumer products company when she discovered a lump in her breast. For two years, it was misdiagnosed until she finally went to a specialist, who told her she had had cancer for two years. "That hit me like a two-by-four," said Lisa. "I had to drive home alone in Hurricane Floyd, from Boston to New York. That was the moment I realized that something had to change: I'm not sure who put the treadmill there, but I'm on it and I have to get off.

"Having breast cancer was the best and worst thing that could ever have happened to me. I tried to take the situation and turn it into something positive." The realities of life don't have to shut down possibilities.

These women were determined survivors who fought against what life handed them, until they had no choice but to stop and regroup. My friend Diane used her time recuperating from a near death car accident to reevaluate her life.

She relived the story: "I lost control of my car on a patch of ice coming down a hill. I hit a guardrail, which broke through the car and through my left leg. I was in the hospital for two months." Diane spent another four months recovering, with steel pins sticking in and out of her legs, surrounded by a cage. She used the time to heal and consider her next steps. She vowed, "I will dance at my fiftieth birthday." She did.

These women interpreted potential tragedy as a signal to stop fighting, start thinking, and begin rescuing themselves.

Not all women experience health crises of this proportion. Sometimes the effect of too much work is the gradual decrease in doing the most basic things, like exercising or eating well. The slow erosion of healthy living is more subtle than the "sledgehammer effect" of serious illness, but it can also lead to its own dire consequences.

Marriage and Motherhood

When Leslie's son was six months old, he had heart surgery. "I left my job for a year and a half trying to rehabilitate him. I had worked since I was fourteen. I was afraid I would never get another job." Taking time off to care for her son gave Leslie time to consider what she had risked by working so hard. "He almost died, and I was not home with him," she said. At the same time, she wondered, How do I keep all these balls in the air? "It's a juggling act. After he got better and I went back to work, it took a year to feel like I wasn't still in a transition."

Peri, whose advertising career was in full swing before she was twenty, hit a roadblock twelve years later. "My daughter was born with an injury. The nerves in her right arm were severed at birth. The doctor told me and my husband that we had to move her arm constantly so that her brain might teach her arm to move. The doctor said, 'She won't be able to shake hands.' Today she swims the butterfly and plays tennis."

Peri had never taken more than two consecutive weeks' vacation in the twelve years she had worked. During her time at home with the baby, it wasn't easy on the economic front. "We were broke, he sells cars, and it was a recession." But she learned how to separate her work and home lives. "I would hate to think that it takes an injured infant or a death, but it's about finding moments in your life. I've learned that working is highly overrated for defining who you are." Peri is a gregarious and confident woman. You'd never guess what she has gone through to get to this point of self-satisfaction.

Marriages also pay the price of overwork. Joan recalled a time when both she and her husband were working at intense jobs and separated by distance. "The only time we saw each other was on the weekends. I would say that I turned off work then, but I was always bringing work with me. Worse, I always worked on vacations. I always flew back for a meeting if there was a major presentation."

Good girls imply or assume that spouses are expected to adopt the same deference to her job demands, even as her job affects the quality of his life and their relationship.

Righting Wrongs

Given their adherence to the rules and personal high standards, we react especially badly to unethical behavior in the office. Because good girls are so committed to doing the right thing, we can be the perfect whistleblowers for abuses of power, unfair decisions, and the illegal business activities too common in twenty-first-century corporations. While someone with a day job attitude might look the other way, many good girls get angry, draw the line, and walk out.

Isa built a successful track record in Silicon Valley. But at one point, she reported to someone who, in her words, was incompetent. She got tangled in a messy incident where he took sides against her and she was put on probation and then fired. That woke her up to realize that her perception of her job as her "calling" wasn't her reality. "I thought I was really making a difference. I guess it was delusional, but if you're working eighty or ninety hours a week, you'd better have a good delusion. I felt betrayed. The next eight months were probably the most miserable of my life."

Julie seethed while her client grew more dictatorial as she "took over" a project that she and Julie had designed together. "I spent these years building this center, but also creating this monster, and it just took the stuffing out of me. I thought I was working for the good guys. I went back to consulting, but new clients just wanted people to give them the answers they wanted. All the things that I was doing to try to make myself happier were just stopgap measures. So I took time off."

Happy Birthday

Birthdays can instigate moments of truth. Monique got her awakening on her fortieth. She was struggling to write a book while running her bed-and-breakfast and editing *Essence* magazine in addition to raising her daughter. "I just didn't see how I was going to add party planning to my list. I started making a big guest list and realized that I didn't have a lot of my friends' addresses. I started crossing everybody's name off one by one (rather than call to find them), and the only name that was left was mine." Monique decided that she'd be the only guest at her party.

She checked herself into a bed-and-breakfast in Cape May, New Jersey, where for a change someone else would take care of her. "I had gotten to the point where I was envious of our guests. I was jealous, even mad at them sometimes. It was difficult to watch them do for themselves what I wasn't doing for myself. I was out on the beach, and I started jotting ideas down for my book about 'having what matters,' and I realized that I couldn't encourage other women to have what matters if I knew inside that I didn't have it."

To echo Monique's feeling, I can't say how many times, while writing this book, I've had to pull myself back from falling into the stress trap again, while writing about taking a break. Even the preachers need a repeat of our own sermons!

Many women have told me that they use their birthdays as "report cards" to evaluate their lives. Birthdays give them reason to ask, Am I happy with my life? The forties and fifties especially are times when women realize how long they've endured a bad situation. "Enough is enough" sums up their resolution to change.

It's not a coincidence that I started my leave on my forty-fifth birthday. I was determined to wake up that day feeling brand new, not just another year older.

Time Off for Happy Reasons

Sometimes there are positive reasons for taking time off. Rather than seek relief or escape, women also pursue personal life-long interests like getting advanced degrees and planning once-in-a-lifetime family adventures. Falling in love and having babies become reasons to stop working and start enjoying life's gifts.

Dreams of faraway places are a lure to leave. Julie spent a year studying in the Far East before she brought her new skills and perspective back home to Washington, D.C. Camille fantasized about living in Italy for a year with her family. Joan wanted to do the same in Paris. Ardith and her husband wanted to trade the Connecticut fast track for the laid-back artistry of Santa Fe. Lisa K. and her husband plotted their escape from New York City to the countryside calm of Vermont. So did Kerry.

At fifty-one, with her two sons grown, Marsha decided to pursue her lifetime love of Jewish music after a successful career spent in technology. Marilyn turned her avocation for the decorative arts to a serious educational focus, also at age fifty-one.

Rosemary got engaged at forty and decided that she'd spend her first year of marriage with her new husband rather than jockeying with her work and travel schedule.

Three of the women had babies late in their thirties. Time off was a chance to learn what motherhood was about after waiting so long for it to happen. After fifteen years of working without a break, both Karen J. and Jane decided to stop and be moms before getting back on their career tracks. Kay, a forty-two-year-old litigator who took time off to spend with her young children after forty, refers to this time as a "pause."

Sharon Hoffman, MBA program director at Stanford Business School, coined the term "stopping out." She calls it a temporary revolving-door decision that has less sense of permanence.[1] According to Sharon, the Stop Outs transfer their passion from work to child-rearing, with every intention of returning to work as the children grow.

We are all searching for the words to capture our need to step away. It's why I used the word "walkabout," which sounded romantic, instead of "leave of absence" or "sabbatical," which feels so clinical. (When I wrote an article about my time off, a magazine editor tried to title it "Diary of a Middle-aged Dropout." I don't know which word upset me more.)

Bored Unhappy

Another consequence of a highly motivated work style is boredom. I don't mean boredom that leads to playing computer games at work, but rather boredom from not satisfying the Type A achievement bug. As aggressive learners, Type A women wither when the learning curve flattens.

In Type A style, Eileen, now fifty-five, recalls her cycles of boredom. "I work hard and fast for about two and a half years, and I finish what I set out to do. If I'm going to re-up in the organization, it's got to be almost another whole plan. The excitement level isn't quite what it was."

Catherine, fifty-one, realized that her career in fashion and marketing had fallen into seven-year cycles. "Maybe there's something to the seven-year itch after all. By the end of the last year, it's as though I felt some gravitational pull telling me that I needed something new, something more."

Joan got her moment of truth on a Monday—actually a series of them. At the retailer where she worked as a top marketer, each week began with "Million-Dollar Monday." "We would spend the whole day reviewing everything that sold, what was good, what was bad. Mondays were always my favorite day, as hellacious as they were."

But after several years of these Monday drills, Joan's passion started to fade. "I found myself sitting there, thinking about retiring early, calculating my bonus. I was sick of the egos, sick of people with bad taste criticizing mine, and sick of defending myself. And I was tired. My daughter was about to go away to boarding school, I realized that in a year it could just be me and my two dogs rambling around my big house. That's when I really started to think about ways to get out."

Donata felt herself get uncomfortable, even in a company she loved. "You know when you're wearing a wool sweater and it just starts to itch? That's how I felt at meetings. I would think, If this were my company, blah, blah, blah. I knew I was I doing a good job and contributing, but I just didn't feel like I belonged anymore."

If you feel that boredom is an unavoidable element in every job, realize that these women are tirelessly ambitious and hungry to learn and grow. Even at the pace they maintain for so many years, they want to be stimulated. They don't quit for easier jobs. They usually move to more challenging ones.

Ignoring the Rescue Squad

I have asked other women whether anyone warned them that they were approaching a breaking point, and they unanimously said "yes," but they didn't listen. Several assumed that their parents or spouses were too sympathetic and didn't understand their "agenda."

Lisa B. noted that colleagues at the office are unable to give you a heads-up when your life goes into a tailspin. "If everybody's as stressed as you are, or working for the same boss in the same environment, it's easy to keep reinfecting the people you work with," she said.

Even when coworkers express sympathy, it's hard to believe they are sincere. Debra remembered that even if she had a cold or was sick, it was common to hear, "Oh, I'm so sorry you feel bad, are you taking anything?" Then, with barely a pause, "Will you still get my report out on time?"

I was also guilty of this bad behavior. Because I was rarely out sick, I was not very sympathetic to people who, in my judgment, "wimped out." If I could get perfect attendance scores, so could they. If I put a new business pitch ahead of my vacation plans, so should they. I had become a nightmare boss and didn't know it.

Bosses are often blind to the escalating frustration that their harsh behavior incites. As one woman put it, "I remember when each time my boss would alight in my doorway, I got stomach cramps. I'd think, What did I do now? Am I in trouble?" Unless you're in a highly humanistic company, your peace of mind and time off isn't at the top of your boss's to-do list. Bottom line results are.

Deborah Holmes, the Americas director of the Center for the New Workforce at Ernst & Young, suggests that women take charge of their own situations. "Nobody is more responsible than you for how your career turns out. If you feel that you're working too hard, it's your turn to say something."

Take your Type A good girl, get-it-done instincts and make yourself the top priority on your to-do list. If you approach your happiness as job one, you might do something about your need for a break.

Waiting for Permission

Waiting for permission to change may be a remnant of one's good girl upbringing. Ann is a case in point. "Basically from 1999 to the end of 2003, I've been at two extremely high-pressure jobs. My husband is out of work, and my mother and father are in and out of hospitals. I have three stepdaughters, and the oldest has Down syndrome. There are times I've been driven to the breaking point, but I haven't given up."

But a year ago, something shifted in Ann's psyche. "I realized I was very depressed. I knew I was overwhelmed and needed help. I felt trapped and I knew it was time to think about the future."

I'll share Ann's resolution in a later chapter, but her moment of truth came when she got her father's blessing to take a break. "I was close to tears when I went to tell my father of my decision. My father was very ill. I knew that I would be making financial sacrifices and my new path might not seem as prestigious. I worried that my father would think I was a flake and irresponsible. I sat down next to his bed, and I told the story. 'You have my blessing, and I'm very proud of you,' he said."

Those were the words Ann most needed to hear. How many times had she feared that he wouldn't support her? Why do we think we are only loved for working hard and doing the "right thing"?

Family reactions carry a lot of weight for good girls. When Monique told her husband she was leaving the magazine to focus on her bed-and-breakfast, her husband was thrilled. She was puzzled when her nine-year-old daughter wasn't. "I was always apologizing to her because I couldn't come to the class play. I was the 'mother who couldn't.' "

Monique told her daughter how she'd be able to pick her up at school and help her with her homework. Instead of being happy, her daughter screamed, "How are we going to have a roof over our head and food on the table?"

"I realized that she had pushed the playback button," said Monique. "Every time I couldn't be there, I would explain, 'Well, you know Mommy has to work, how else are we going to have a roof over our heads and food on the table?' "

Though we can turn a deaf ear to family members' concerns about our overwork, sometimes their words break through as A-ha moments. Liz remembered, "I had a complete revelation one day. I was still at Nike, and my brother Brendan said that he had tried for over a month to reach me by phone, and I was never home. So he said, 'I ran a LexisNexis search on you to see if I could figure out where you were.' Isn't that the most awful thing you've ever heard in your whole life? That was a major turning point when my own brother said that he was searching worldwide databases to figure out where his sister was.

"My life is so the opposite of that now," laughs Liz. "Now I talk to my siblings every single day. I've overcorrected." (Starting a national talk radio program with her four sisters is an example of how far a Type A will go to right a situation.)

Who Am I Without My Job?

Since good girls identify so closely with their jobs, the fear of stepping away can be paralyzing. The rhythm of working life has an iron grip on us. We think of our colleagues as our friends. We mark our identity on our business cards. We wonder, Who will I be if I'm not working?

As Kay considered whether to leave her law firm, one of her worries was separating from her "real friends" at work. "What will I do when I can't come here every day and say hi to Sara and go to lunch?" she wondered. "Work was the fun part of my life, even if it was giving me stress."

To justify our dedication, we glorify the good parts of work and deny what's eating at us. Kay had hung on to her assignments as a trial lawyer for the challenge, but she had to face the reality of what her job had become over time. "At the office, most people my age had already gone on to other things," she said. "I realized that I was winding down. It seemed so overwhelming to keep my clothes in the closet clean, so I could get up in the morning and get dressed. I just felt like I had way too much to do."

Our jobs can overtake our identity, especially if we've adopted a corporate persona and forgotten who we really are apart from work. Isa was a buttoned-up leader of a customer service team at a high-tech company by day and a freestyle dancer by night. "My nonintegrated life was driving me crazy. Half my life, I'm this goody-two-shoes corporate girl, and the other half, I'm this totally wild, self-expressed, vivacious woman, dancer, and artist who doesn't fit the norms. I felt conflicted every moment. There were gut-wrenching feelings in my stomach and in my body. Even though I was living in a great place and had money, I had no sense of self at all."

Leaving a job title behind, warts and all, is like walking away from who you are, who you've worked to become. It took me time to realize that the corner office and all that came with it became my shorthand for who I was, as if being CEO of an ad agency endowed me with worth or engendered instant respect. Now that I have stepped away from my "old life," it's amazing to me how much more satisfying it is to be respected for what I have learned rather than for the title on my business card.

Letting go of the rituals and relationships of your day-to-day work isn't easy, until you experience life on "the other side." Marcia Worthing, a veteran human resources executive who regularly counsels people who've been fired, describes the step by step of letting office relationships and identity go. "They've left their companies and realize that nobody cares they've left. Soon they start to realize that they don't care, either. They stop thinking about what's happening there, or caring about the gossip or even the earnings. They put it into perspective, and they see that a company is a company. It's not a friend, or a family member. You don't love it. It's just a place that you were able to work and contribute. You get a better sense of what's important and what's not."

A good friend of mine helped me understand this concept. She said that when it comes time to leave a job, it's not that you are wrong or that the company is wrong. For many years, your goals were aligned. But at some points, your paths diverge. You each move on as individual entities, glad for the time you had together.

Getting Control of Your Stress

Rather than wait for the A-ha moment to hit, we can build in more frequent mental temperature checks. When I worked at the ad agency, I used to do a little self-evaluation quiz I called the Mirror Test, to bring sanity to my chaotic days. Each night, I would ask myself three questions, "Did I do the right thing for the agency's people?" "For the agency's clients?" "And for our creative product?" If I could answer "yes" to all three, I could call it a day and feel I'd done the best I could.

Unfortunately, one question was never on that list: "Did I do the right thing for me?" I never seemed important enough to rate a spot on the quiz. If I had asked, maybe I would have taken that time off a lot sooner.

It's important to create ongoing checkups that douse the burnout before it gets out of hand. Birthdays are a natural annual time for reflection. Ask yourself the simplest questions, such as, "Am I happy to go to work in the morning?" "How would I grade myself on the time I spend with my family?"

Another way to ward off impending burnout is to invite exercise back onto your calendar. Though many of the women I met joked about how they had stopped working out due to mounting responsibilities, the effect of exercise as a stress reliever is no laughing matter. In her Washington *Post* article "De-Stress Yourself," Carol Krucoff writes that "staying healthy in a high-pressure world requires adopting strategies to relieve tension and counter the damaging effects of chronic stress."[2]

She quotes Michael H. Sacks, professor of psychiatry at Cornell University Medical College in New York, who ties the benefits of exercise to both physical and mental health. "Exercise acts as a buffer against stress and can help protect the cardiovascular and immune systems from the consequences of stressful events. Regular exercise is an effective treatment for anxiety, and according to some research, is as effective as psychotherapy in treating mild or moderate depression."[3]

Shifting from the treadmill of your job to the one in the gym could be your way of taking control of your runaway stress.

Taking a Preemptive Time Off

Goal-setting and planning comes naturally to good girls. Take a weekend once a quarter, or set aside one Saturday or Sunday, which you spend alone. Don't clean out the closet or write e-mails to friends. Feel what that downtime feels like, without the pressure of pleasing others or the urgency to complete tasks. Ask yourself, What are the top three changes I'd like to make that would make my life happier? If your job situation or an overloaded calendar is one of them, that's a moment of truth that you can begin to act on.

If you are feeling, Oh, I couldn't take a whole weekend to myself, that's an indication of just how far you are overindexing on meeting everyone else's needs. How many Saturdays do the men in your life play golf for five hours? (If you do it, too, good for you!) How many weekends do you shuttle your kids to every possible sporting event? How many days do you drop your own plans to help a friend, visit parents, or just attend a series of summer barbeques? Isn't your happiness, health, and passion worthy of the same energy? There are fifty-two weekends a year to choose from. Claim at least one of them as your own.

No Time to Rest

Still, many women will shake their heads, saying, "I can't deal with this decision now. How about later?" They're literally too busy to rest.

Monique has an answer for them. "Most of us get busy being busy so that we don't have to face these difficult questions. It's not easy to change your life. We avoid it by filling up all our time. Time off doesn't take a week or five weeks or five months. If we give ourselves to ourselves on a daily basis, then the process doesn't have to be so overwhelming."

Monique acknowledged that, before her leave, she wasn't conscious of how she was living her daily life. "Now I'm trying to have that discussion with myself every day so it doesn't have to be this big epiphany. I'm always checking in with me."

She's got an everyday process that works for her. Even though she wakes up around 6:30 A.M., she doesn't get out of bed for about twenty minutes or so. She lays there quietly, thinking through her day, sensing how she's feeling. If sitting cross-legged and *Ohm*-ing seems too confining for Type A energy, this reclining morning meditation might work instead.

I've listened to many women try to solve problems by worrying about them instead of facing them. I believe that good girls try to silently mull their way out of a rut, figuring if they just work harder, it will solve itself.

Dr. Naomi Swanson, supervisory research psychologist at the National Institute for Occupational Safety and Health, analyzes women's problem-solving process this way: "Women tend to use emotion-focused strategies, like seeking social support. But self-blame or avoidance or denial, that's called rumination, chewing on something over and over again. That actually increases the amount of stress and contributes to poor health."

Lisa B. painted the grim picture of how that "chewing" paralyzes action. She described her train of thought on a typical morning. "You're going to work, riding up in that same elevator that you've ridden for the last five years and facing the same levels of stress and somehow feeling that you're trapped and that without that job, you will literally be living a horrible life in some fleabag apartment. And all the fears are completely ridiculous. Fear was what kept me from going somewhere else. You're afraid to leave and you're staying out of fear, too. But it's not that scary once you cross over, and you're really not going to be destitute if you leave."

Listen to Your Inner Voice

You can force your own moment of truth by stopping and listening to the voice inside you. As good girls, we discount the importance of our own voices, or we silently berate ourselves to "buck up" or "get over it." Being sympathetic and respectful to our own feelings is a new behavior to learn. And listen to the voices of those who truly love you. In a high-pressure environment, we give more credit to our critics, our colleagues, our bosses than to the people who know us best.

Dr. Redford Williams, director of the Behavioral Medicine Research Center at Duke University Medical Center, suggests that listening is a skill that overachieving Type A women may need to develop. "The women you're talking about here may not be the best of listeners. They may be more used to getting their messages across."

I felt the sting of what he said. We "sell" ourselves on why it makes sense to overindex on work. We rationalize why we need to postpone our own needs. We aren't listening because we want to be right. It's ironic that at Just Ask a Woman, I base my success on how well I listen to women. In my personal life, I've been accused of being a half listener. I finish other's sentences because I believe I know where they are heading, a long-held Type A trait. Learning to listen fully, to others and to myself, is a real challenge.

Dr. Williams describes the benefits of better listening. "Being a good listener is a very effective way to establish more supportive relationships. Research shows that this kind of coping skills training, being able to manage negative situations, shows reduced stress hormones and improved immune function." The physiological benefits are interesting. But the psychological benefits of enjoying a more connected life can be the key to helping you manage your stress and avoid relapse.

Taking the Leap

Waiting for the perfect plan may mean you'll never face the music. When Cindy quit her job to deliver the eulogy at her friend's memorial service, she didn't have a plan. "I packed as much as I could into a cardboard box, and I walked out at lunchtime. I called the office and said, 'I'm having a family emergency.' I didn't lie. I was my family and I was having an emergency." Cindy is a calm woman who doesn't storm out or make rash decisions. For once, though, she listened to the voice inside her that said it was time to go.

Your opportunity may come as a result of the jolt of being fired or the gift of getting a package, through a sabbatical program at your company or being "let off the hook" by someone you care about, or just by running away from it all. The moment of truth comes when you're ready to hear it. Whenever I was asked how I dared to walk away, it's usually preceded with "Weren't you scared?" or "You were so brave!" I always answered, "I just stopped banging my head against the wall." The decision to give yourself a break can be as simple as that.

The A-ha Moment: Lisa B.'s Story

Lisa B. was thirty-five, single, and well regarded in her fast-paced online travel company. A determined go-getter, she had worked since she was fourteen, trained by hard-charging parents to compete and succeed. She might still be working at a breakneck pace to prove to them and to herself that she was an independent success story if it weren't for a startling moment of truth. I met Lisa in Florida, just as she had finished a year that was partly on and mostly off.

Lisa's A-ha story traced back to when she was twenty-one. "As college ended, I went to Europe for the summer and worked in a hotel. I fell madly in love with Mauro, this man I met in Italy. Two months later, just as I was starting my job with Hyatt in Chicago, Mauro came to the States to see me. We were going to spend a month together to find out if it was true love. But when he arrived, I had no time for him."

In the few short months since their summertime romance, Lisa had become a different person than the carefree woman who was cleaning rooms by day, drinking champagne by night. "In Chicago, I was working twelve- to fourteen-hour days and this poor man was in my apartment waiting for me to come home. When I did, I was so tired that I didn't have the energy to do anything but literally crawl into bed and go to sleep. So he went his way, and I went mine."

Lisa's story fast-forwards fourteen years to Dallas, where she'd relocated for another travel job. Her Italian friend staged a second surprise visit. He arrived to spend two weeks in Dallas to see if they could rekindle their relationship.

At this stage of her career, thirty-five-year-old Lisa's work calendar had grown even more intense, so much so that she felt intolerant of his presence, even though she cared about him and even though she was still unattached.

"After only a few days, I was ready to put him back on the plane," she said. "I felt that rising impatience and frustration, and I recalled having those very same feelings in Chicago twelve years earlier."

Even though she felt guilty to be wishing him away, Lisa's good girl reaction was to rationalize her overwork. She counseled herself, "Don't get hung up on the fact that the same thing is happening again. That's not a problem. You're making a ton of money, you own your condo. Life is good."

Lisa's next strategy was to shift the blame to Mauro: "Why did he show up without warning? I just don't have time for these kinds of things. Somebody comes into my life for two weeks to stay with me after fourteen years? I mean, what a huge imposition that was!"

Blaming others for the style of our work lives is easy. We pass the buck for our out-of-control agendas, by protesting, "My business is insanely busy this time of year." "I've got a really tough boss." We make excuses, rather than admitting, "I am overworked and I have to do something about it." That way, we don't have to make a greater admission: "I am lonely."

Dr. Kaye Moore says that when women are in denial, "it takes enormous internal resources to push stuff down, and that is why many women are absolutely exhausted. We're using all our energy not to see what it is that we don't want to see."

It's true that Lisa was exhausted. Her long hours and Type A ambition were draining her life. Even at the end of a long day, she said, "It took every bit of energy not to get back on e-mail, not check my voice mail, and I worked on weekends, too. That lifestyle really isolated me, even from myself."

Lisa's salvation came just as she was facing off with her Italian beau in a blinding sequence of imaginary scenes that she calls her Scrooge moment. In the Charles Dickens story, Ebenezer Scrooge has three visions over the course of Christmas Eve, where in a dream he sees his past, his present, and his future. Similarly, three "ghosts" appeared to Lisa.

Lisa's eyes widened as she returned to that moment. "Suddenly I had this flashback, when you go back in time very quickly, and Mauro became the boyfriend of the past.

The same scene, but back in Chicago. And then my mind returned to the present, and I was looking at the reality of my life. While I acknowledged that some big positives had happened in my life, I asked, What hasn't changed? I'm still exhausted. I'm over-worked. I don't have a relationship. I don't have children. And then suddenly—it was like a split second—I went fast-forward, and real-ized, Oh my God, he could come back ten years from now and what will have changed then?"

As we race through our lives, how often do we stop to compare our lives of five or ten years ago to now . . . and then project five or ten years forward? How many of us can easily recite the long-term objectives for our businesses, yet we are delinquent about planning our personal lives? We rarely pause to ask if we are in a rut, or repeat-ing patterns of behavior we don't like, or set an end zone when we will stop charging on. And without a serious analysis of what behav-iors we might want to change, we are likely to confront a future that's a twin to our current situation.

Lisa was lucky. The appearance of her "ghost boyfriend" made her look at her present life. She silently asked herself, "What's not working in my life? What about the fact that I'm still not in a happy relationship? That I am not connected to any of my friends like I used to be? What about having a baby? It wasn't even on my radar."

Lisa projected forward by ten years and was shocked to realize, "In ten years, I'll be forty-five and what are my chances of having a baby then?" She scolded herself, "You like this life? You stick with it and in ten years, you're going to be grumpier. You're going to be more tired. And you're going to be alone. So do you really want to look at life right now and call it his fault?"

Lisa was in tears as she told me this story. The effect of that past-present-future revelation was that she finally saw the truth of what she had to do to change her future. In a stroke of unusual pluck, she skipped work and booked tickets to San Francisco for her and her friend to try to make up for lost time. There she got another "sign." "I woke up with this really weird sensation. I picked up my phone and I heard a message from my mom. She said, 'I just had this strange feeling about you, and I want to call because I know you're stressed. I know that you want to make changes in your life. And I just want to let you know that, no matter what, I love you very much and no matter what you decide to do, I will take care of you. You can come back home.' "

It was the approval that Lisa needed. "I was all alone, and I felt I didn't have anybody in my life. My dad's dead. And the one person in my life that I needed permission from was giving it to me, because that's whom I wanted to please. That's why this whole thing started. I wanted to make my parents proud. I needed to know that if I stepped over that ledge and left my job, I wasn't going to drown. I had her permission and her acceptance. That meant as much to me as my own revelation."

She returned to Dallas and made the decision to reclaim her life. "I'll never forget. I called Mauro and said that I had quit. And he said, 'Great, I'll come pick you up,' because he thought I meant I'd quit early for the day. I packed up all my stuff and I was standing there waiting for him in the parking lot like a schoolgirl. I got in the car, with tears streaming down my face, and he looked at me strangely, as if to say, 'She's getting off early and she's crying . . . what's going on?' "

"And I said, 'I quit.' He was still confused and asked, 'But what is "quit"?' And I yelled, 'Quit! Quit! Finito! Or whatever.' There was this huge sense of relief, like somebody had just picked off that huge safe that I had on top of my back."

Lisa took a year to recoup and to experiment with different jobs, even different cities. She isn't in a romantic relationship with Mauro, but they are still good friends. "Our friendship remains and our connection actually increased as a result of his participation in what has been the most significant bucking of the system I've successfully accomplished to date." She's still in transition, but happy to have left her lifeless, overworked routine. "They could give me half a million dollars and I swear I wouldn't take it."

Her advice to other women? "Because of that incredible unveiling of my attitudes, it was like somebody just cleared the smoke out of my reality. Before that moment, I had no idea there was any smoke there. And that's the moment that I want to see women experience. If you're knee-level or waist-level or neck-level into whatever you're doing, what will be that Scrooge moment for you?"

YOUR MOMENT OF TRUTH

Has your moment of truth already happened, and if so, describe it as if it were a scene in a film. _____

_____

_____

_____

Has this moment happened more than once?   _____

_____

Whose permission do you think you need to take a break? _____

_____

_____

Ghostwrite a letter from that person to you, supporting your decision to do it. _____

_____

_____

_____

Is there a negative sound track playing in your head, telling you all the reasons you couldn't take time off? Write it out and change the lyrics. _____

_____

_____

_____

What I Love to Do and Am Uniquely Good At	What I Hate to Do and Am Not Very Good At

As you look at this chart, how does the right side of the page make you feel? _____

_____

Are there things on the right side that you do every day in your job?

_____

How would you feel if you never had to do them again?   _____

_____

_____

Look at the left side of the page. How does that side make you feel?

_____

_____

Which things on there could you imagine incorporating into your life as you live it now? _____

_____

Which ones would require a change in your job or your schedule?

_____

_____

What would it take to make those happen? _____

_____

_____

Draw a pie chart of how you are spending your days. Include everything: work, commuting, exercise, time with family and friends, spiritual time, sleep, intellectual nourishment, entertainment, and mindless fun.

Then draw an ideally proportioned chart that reflects the way you'd like to live your life, and see how your "real life" chart compares. (A horribly unmatched pie tells you that it's time to reassess your job and your personal priorities.)

If you were to make a change and take a break, list three people you can depend on for unwavering, unpressured support.

1. _____
2. _____
3. _____

List three people who are likely to squash your hopes of changing your life.

1. _____
2. _____
3. _____

Write the answer you would say to them if they were facing you right now with their doubts. _____
_____
_____

CHAPTER SIX

What Time Off Feels Like

If you threw away your commuter train schedule, dodged the morning rush-hour traffic, tossed away your "to do" cramped days and overtime nights, muffled the demands of your boss, and walked away from the frustration that wears you down... imagine the blank space left for your life.

Until you take time off, you may have a hard time crystallizing what that wonderful emptiness feels like. Think of how good it feels to step out of high heels when you walk through your door at night. Tune in to that early morning silence when you awaken before anyone else. Smell the air when it's not clogged with bus exhaust. Taste what food tastes like when it's not wolfed down. Now you're starting to feel what it feels like to take back your life.

When I awoke on my first day off, I almost laughed out loud. I yelled, "I'm free!" before I even got out of bed. I had just turned forty-five, but I felt like I was ten. I had only a vague sense of what I'd do. Only you can design your own time off. Perhaps these stories will inspire you.

Time to Travel

While you may want to pull the covers over your head and nap your way through your break, exotic travel may meet your needs for escape. Joan got her idea for her year-long leave in Paris from a book called *Without Reservations: The Travels of an Independent Woman.* "It's about a woman who turns fifty," said the newly fifty Joan. "She suddenly moved to Paris but knew if she was going to take time off, she couldn't just plop down and be a lady of leisure. So she set up a routine. I became obsessed with this idea."

Paris was a city that Joan had always loved, but had only visited in short bursts during business trips. "One night, I said to my husband, 'Wouldn't you just love to move to Paris?' And he said, 'That's what I love about you, you're always open to something exciting. That's exactly what we should do.' I don't know if he was kidding, but I took him seriously. Within the next thirty days, that was it."

As she started to make plans, she realized that her dream of personal escape turned into a mission to make a wonderful experience for her family. She enrolled her daughter in school there, rented a small apartment for the three of them, and set up her own "routine" of cooking classes, French lessons, art history, and drawing (her Type A tendencies were in evidence here). Her husband's job gave him geographic flexibility, so each of them was able to enjoy the year.

Her favorite memories were of long dinners with friends. "Dinner parties in Paris would start at eight P.M. and we'd just sit around the dinner table and talk until one A.M. when we'd have our last coffee and say good night. I will have those friends for the rest of my life. I feel like I have a worldview like I never had. I relaxed. I lived."

For Camille, tossing the routine was a critical piece of her rest from the high-pressure world of publicity. She chose Italy as the destination for her time off with her family. "I love routine, but it was good for me to get pulled out of mine. Everything was different. I was nervous, but it was good for me."

Camille left her job for five months to live in an apartment in the historic center of Rome with her husband and her two children. "The kids started school. I took Italian lessons. I joined a walking group run by an American historian, so I did tons of exploring and shopping. Even mundane errands were an excuse to get inside the fabric of the city. I had more time with my husband and my kids because we were so removed from the world."

This short time period led her to focus on the quality of how she spent her days. "Once we knew we had only a month left, we didn't waste it. If we met someone we liked, we invited them over to dinner right away."

Camille returned to her former position to find that some people didn't realize she had been gone. "The difference was more inside me," she said. "It reconfirmed what was important in life, namely friends and family. Many of my friends say they are going to do great things when they retire. Why wait? I feel so lucky we did it when the kids could benefit."

Camille concludes, "I continue to tell anyone who asks that our time in Rome was truly the best thing we've ever done for our family and for all of us as individuals. As time passes, I realize more and more what an extraordinary gift that sabbatical was and how it will forever be in all of our minds, a magical, perfect time."

Julie left her government consulting job for a trip to the Far East. Her time off started in a thunderstorm of anxiety. "It was pouring the day I left from my mother's house in New Jersey. I had this horrific bus ride to JFK Airport for my New York–Korea–Australia flight, thinking, It can't get any worse than this! When I arrived in Australia, my friend and I went to this youth hostel called something like the Pink House. There I was, thirty-five years old, with my backpack, staring into this youth hostel filled with nineteen-year-old guys with dreadlocks, and thinking, What have I done?"

Once she relaxed after a few weeks in Australia, Julie moved on to Asia. She started studying kickboxing after she had been mugged a year and a half before, so she followed her love for martial arts to China. "I spent six weeks with monks in the Shaolin Temple, studying kung fu eight hours a day, seven days a week." She also became a Reiki healer in Thailand. (Again, Type A fever to achieve strikes while resting.)

Julie's Reiki training had a long-lasting effect. She notices that when she's in a tense situation, she can literally cool down the emotional temperature in the room. "When tempers are rising, I automatically say, 'Wait, let's step back a bit.' I'm not so sure that it had to do with traveling as much as it did with taking the time out to rediscover who I was and who I am and who I can be," she concludes.

While hardworking businesswomen are used to travel, their schedules are usually determined by others' needs and timing. A benefit of taking time off is the gift of spontaneity, the ability to travel when *you* want.

After Liz quit, she got a chance to see what travel on her own terms felt like. "A friend of mine was getting married in Switzerland, so I actually got to go to her wedding. It was normally the kind of thing I would have missed or only been able to come in for a day but miss all the fun. It was great to be able to be there for all five days of festivities."

Later, a close friend of hers invited her to come to Bangkok for the winter. Liz's reflex was to turn him down. "I remember saying, 'I can't come to Bangkok to stay for two or three months!' And then I hung up and I realized, 'Yes I can!' Right after Thanksgiving, I went to Thailand for two and a half months, first living at Marc's and then traveling around the region."

We don't often get to drop our responsibilities and take off for far-flung places. But time off teaches us what it feels like to be spontaneous, perhaps for the first time.

Joan, Camille, Julie, and Liz had something in common. They had money put aside so that they could handle the expense of travel, and they worked their finances so that they could live within their means overseas. All four women traveled because they wanted to experience other cultures to stretch out of their nine-to-five lives. If you want to immerse yourself in a new culture, then you might plan this kind of time off. But exotic travel is a bad idea if you're just running away from your problems.

Lisa B. is an example of travel gone wrong. She had quit without any plan other than to get away from her oppressive job. "I called my mom the next day and said, 'What am I going do?' And she said,

'You've been out of work for twelve hours and you're already trying to figure out your next career?' "

In an effort to take some kind of action, Lisa took her mother and a friend on a long-promised trip to Mexico right away. It was too soon, and too crowded with everyone else's interests. "I needed time alone," she said. "Instead I was with my mother and her friend. I even tried to start up a jewelry importing business while I was down there. I wanted to jump right into replacing work, like it was a drug."

When she returned home, she wasn't relaxed or resolved. "So I ran off to Europe. It was probably the fight-or-flight deal," she said. Unfortunately, Lisa discovered that her worries didn't evaporate when she landed overseas. "I was miserable," she recalled. "No matter where I was or what I did, my worry about what to do next was gnawing away at me." She came back sooner than planned and started the hard work of figuring out the rest of her life.

Starting right in to solve your stress on day one of a break is asking for trouble. Dr. Redford Williams of the Duke University Medical Center suggests that you make your career planning its own separate agenda. "During the break, I'd say just go out and have fun and lie on the beach, if you could force yourself to do it. Relax, get away, and don't think about work. But taking care of the stresses you have on a day-to-day basis is whole other initiative." He advises setting aside separate time to examine what caused the stress and how you might cope with it differently, so that when you return you don't repeat the situation you left behind. Travel is only a good option if you are starting the trip on solid footing.

Time to Stay Home and Be Mom

Not everyone packed a suitcase and bolted for the wild blue yonder. Jane, who made the plan to leave her teaching job for a year to stay home with her four-year-old daughter, Katie, found her oasis in the simple things she had forgotten in her hectic life as a teacher.

"It was the best year of my life," she said. "It's when I started enjoying mornings."

Jane's own mom had taken her to her first day of school. Although Katie was happy in day care, Jane would not let a stranger replace her on that important day, so she took her year off when Katie started preschool. "I took Katie to her first day, and she said, 'You're not leaving, right?' and I said, 'No, I'm going to sit out in the parking lot the whole time you're here.' Jane returned in time for recess, and as the children came outside, she watched Katie do a double take. "I went to pick her up every day that year and once I heard her say to someone, 'Oh, my mom waits all day in the parking lot every day.' She still thinks I did."

Jane learned what it felt like to live in her own life. "I could just be the mom. Sometimes Katie and I would just go to the store or the park. We went to the beach in the winter. I went to every one of my stepson Brian's basketball games and they went all the way to the state championship. I read books. I rarely if ever read books for pleasure during the school year. I made every Christmas gift I gave to friends and neighbors. I often went downtown to the Italian market in Philadelphia on a weekday and shopped for great pastas and fruits and vegetables. We went as a family to Disney World— in November, not in the middle of summer like all teachers do. I did all of the things I normally would have done on the weekend or on vacation."

Katie also learned some lessons from her mother's time off. "When she grows up and chooses to work, or to be the mom, she's learned that you can have downtime. The most important thing is that you love your life."

Jane's insight matched the findings of a major study by Ellen Galinsky, president of the Families and Work Institute. Most children, when asked what they would change about their frazzled parents, didn't choose the number of hours that their parents worked, but rather that their parents wouldn't be so stressed. In her book *Ask the Children*, Galinsky points to the value of ritual and routines, rather than fancy vacations, as the solution for children's needs.[1]

Like Jane, Kay and Karen J. had their children when they were in their late thirties. Kay left her job because she was pulled in too many directions and wanted to spend more time with her children. "I notice at the nursery school that there's this confluence of women my age, who are at the last moment having children. Some of them are doing what I'm doing. In a sense I'm not in transition. I'm able to just do what my mother did for me. There's a lot in it for the children to have a parent who is available all the time."

Kay is one of millions of mothers who are choosing to take time for a while to be stay-at-home moms. Recent articles in major media are touting the tug-of-war that moms feel between their jobs and their children. Despite the stories of high-profile women who take a few years off to be with their kids, the Census Bureau says that 72 percent of mothers work.[2] There is a slight decline in that percentage among "older mothers" age thirty to thirty-four and more educated women, who are less likely to return to work.[3] Despite the coverage of a major opt-out trend, the truth is that most moms need or want to keep working, which is why so many companies have had to address their stress with programs, like extended maternity leave. The pattern of "sequencing," where women go in and out of the workforce during a career, is becoming more common. In a study from Catalyst, if women who are not mothers are factored out, the actual rate of sequencing professionals approaches 50 percent.[4]

As much as she is glad for her time as a mom, the trial lawyer in Kay still wrestles with the stay-home/go-to-work argument. "I still feel the isolation of my situation. But I no longer feel like I have to justify it to anybody." Kay refers to her time at home as a "pause" rather than retirement.

Karen J. explained her feelings about staying home due to a later pregnancy. "If I had had Sophie at twenty-five, I would have felt tremendous pressure to be supermom, superwife, and supercareer woman. By the time I was thirty-eight, I had achieved a lot in my profession, and I just wanted to be a mom for a while. It took me a long time to have a baby and trying to get pregnant was almost like having a second job.

"What I needed was to enjoy being a mom, and I did not want to miss her being a baby. I loved focusing only on Sophie. I was fortunate to have been able to stop and spend the time that I did. Who benefited? We both did, but I remember the time I spent with her and she doesn't, so I would say that I was the big winner."

Karen ultimately took two years off and then went back to a freelance version of her production career, and still maintains a flexible parenting schedule with her husband, Paul. "I could never give up being part of Sophie's growing up once I'd felt what it felt like to be there every day," concludes Karen.

When her own mother died, Debra felt even more desire to spend time with her own children. "I have taken the time to mourn my personal loss and put in perspective the values my mother gave me and how I can do the same for my children," she said. "My children are thrilled to have their mother as a more active part of their lives, yet still understand that they are part of but not all of my life and activities."

Time to Create

A break is also a way to unleash creativity. Isa, the computer whiz by day and dancer named Glitter Girl by night, opened the Temple of Poi, a studio to teach fire dancing. Donata opened herself up to a wider career that spans appearances on TV as an entertainment expert, magazine and book author, and developed a product line under her name with 1800Flowers.com.

Karen N., who left her high-level fashion marketing job to stay home with her new baby, found herself wearing an oversize T-shirt postpregnancy. As a solution, she created what would become a line of best-selling pajamas for women. (This is what happens when a Type A overachiever sits around in her PJs.) Karen admitted that she'd never have come up with her new business if she hadn't taken the time off. "I never would have had the time or the inclination.

I guess I always had the desire, but it was totally buried under all this other work I had to do."

Karen N. is not alone as a female entrepreneur. It's a fact that 48 percent of all privately held businesses in the U.S. are owned 50 percent or more by women, according to the Center for Women's Business Research.[5]

Since staying home, Kay decided to take her knitting hobby online, by designing a knitting website with her friend, who's also an at-home mom. "We're the world's only two-headed blog," she said. "We write letters to each other. For people who are into the world of knitting, we're famous. Not famous like Frank Sinatra, but like Deborah Kerr famous."

When Lisa K. moved to Vermont with her family, she and a friend launched Artemis Woman, a wellness company that creates skin and therapeutic products for women. She was inspired by her own learning experience from breast cancer. Her well-honed marketing skills from her former big company job helped her sell over thirty-five thousand units of one of her products on QVC in one day.

While home with her child in Vermont, Kerry used her PR smarts to start a fashion accessories business with a product called Take Outs or, in her words, "fake boobs." She is already creating her next new line of accessories.

A particular result of moms getting time to be moms is that they start businesses that solve the problems of motherhood. Well-known designer Liz Lange started a line of designer maternity clothes once her friends experienced the wardrobe horror show of pregnancy. BlueSuitMom.com is a helpful website for working moms, started by Maria Bailey after she went through the challenge of balancing work with raising four children.

Time off is meant to be off, but once you get some time to breathe, you will find that your natural talents and passions reemerge . . . and sometimes give birth to a new life, one more aligned with your newly uncovered priorities.

Time to Learn

When I started my time off, the first thing I did was register for dancing lessons. Every New Year, dancing was on my list of resolutions, so the leave seemed the perfect time to make it happen. Other women also decided to use time off for learning. Ardith took singing lessons. Camille and Joan studied languages. As part of her arrangement to secure her sabbatical, Jane took additional credits in psychology.

But some women used their leaves purely for educational pursuits. Marilyn, who left her twenty-five-year career in real estate law at fifty, took a year to decide what she wanted to do. "When you're older and you do this, you do have a certain amount of credibility and capability that's recognized by other people."

Since she had always been interested in contemporary crafts and antiques, she enrolled in decorative arts courses at The New School in New York City. "It wasn't as if I was taking one course. That would have driven me nuts. I decided to go for a master's in the history of decorative arts." That spurred four years of study and a thesis, which evolved into a book she wrote, called *Selling Good Design: Promoting the Early Modern Interior.*

Marilyn's advice for those who decide to study while off (especially if they have been out in the workforce for years)? "Don't be afraid to go back to school. Our brains are still quite capable of absorbing new information, even after estrogen depletion." Marilyn, who's now fifty-eight, also suggests that other women her age see that "there may be careers that were not open to us, or did not even exist, when we were making career decisions in our twenties."

Time off can be a way to pick up an earlier love that may have been postponed over the course of a life. Marsha, fifty-five, former president of a technology company in Upper Montclair, New Jersey, had studied music in college, even been awarded two master's degrees in it. After a detour into a successful television career, she continued toward her Ph.D. and was two thirds of the way through when she stopped her education short a second time, due to costs and events in her personal life. Instead, she went on to integrate a second successful career in technology with her family's needs, and put her nearly completed dissertation aside.

She had maintained a journal for twenty-five years as a source of daily meditation. "This habit helped me come to the realization that the dissertation would always be unfinished business for me and that I'd always feel a sense of incompletion without it." She took a "quasi-self-imposed" sabbatical, as she puts it, and rented an apartment in Princeton and sequestered herself three days a week to finish her Ph.D. in music at the university. "When the dean of the graduate school shook my hand, I felt a great sense of fulfillment."

"I've learned so much, even beyond the doctoral degree," said Marsha. "Time is indeed a gift. What matters . . . changes. Not having children at home anymore enabled me to enjoy not working for the first time in my adult life. Time off allowed me the space to see what works for me now. I love the 'casserole' of my life." (In short order, Marsha went from being a successful technology entrepreneur to a composer, lecturer, and performer of Jewish music. A truly Type A comeback for a woman who started a birthday party entertaining business at age twelve with only a guitar.)

Time to Be Friends

In the contest between work and friends, friends often lose. We can all recall the personal invitations over the years that are forfeited for work. Even simple things like having drinks with friends or attending baby showers fall second to work, or compete with scarce personal time. Time off is a real eye opener to what we could be doing if we were in control of our lives.

Cindy, who quit so that she could give a proper memorial to her friend who had died, said, "I did not go on a big travel jaunt because I felt that a good way of honoring him would be to be a better friend to the people who were still here.

"One of my best friends was pregnant at the time with her fourth child," Cindy continues. "So I spent a lot of time with her and with her other kids. I spent a week with a friend whose husband died. I spent time with a woman whose father had died. She was sitting shivah for the first time in her life. Dealing with death may not be as interesting as going to Hawaii, but it was meaningful to me.

"Now I have become thought of, not as the person who is always stressed out by their work, but as the extra parent who is available to do things to help my friends," she said. "I'm available to pick up my friends' kids from school if they need a break. Sometimes I've gotten off track and I have to remind myself that being a good friend is a really valuable role to play."

According to Dr. Kaye Moore, before we can even reach out to others, we need to connect with ourselves. "If you are not connected with yourself, you cannot connect with anyone else on the planet—period—your family, your community, whatever. You must give yourself priority." Kay told me that this comment is usually met with silence, then laughter. Women know that they are so far from behaving this way. We have to practice being friends again.

Time to Fall in Love

Two women learned that they were able to open up to new love in their lives after getting out from under the yoke of the crazy hours. At age fifty-five, Lalita, who's never been married, just got engaged. She believes that only time off allowed her to make that kind of life commitment. Instead of having to be in control, she was able to let go and welcome someone else into her life. "Without retooling my brain, I don't think I could have met this wonderful man or even considered hooking up with someone else, because a relationship means that you have to consider their wishes, too."

Lalita's description of sharing control is a tribute to the hardest part of Type A determination—letting go.

Terry, who was single and childless when she was working in an investment management company in San Francisco, shared these frustrations. While she felt that married women and moms both felt job pressure, "When you're single, they don't think any excuse to leave work is good enough. The managers knew they couldn't control women's day-care problems. But my nonprofit volunteering wasn't a good enough excuse."

Shortly after she left her job at age forty-two for a two-year "trip around the world," she met the man she would marry. "There's no way I would have gotten married if I were still there," she said. "I usually just annoyed people because I was never available to them." Now she's a forty-five-year-old bride.

Terry also talked of another kind of love, which only animal lovers might understand. "When I was working so many hours, I wasn't even good to my dog," she said. "What I most enjoyed was the time I spent with my dog, Holly. I traveled up and down the West Coast with her even though she was getting older. During that time, I finally had to put her to sleep. I never could have lived with myself if I'd done it when I was working and neglecting her."

Courtney bought a puppy during her time off. So did Ardith. So did I. As Courtney said, "There's nothing like a puppy to give you perspective on life." Beside the obvious companionship, I think there are two other reasons that time off inspires us to invite pets into our lives. A pet is a symbol of life outside of work, especially for childless women. And having an eager and innocent pup greet you at the door is a constant reminder of the value of unconditional love, unlinked to any job performance or status.

Time off isn't a guarantee for finding a love life—canine or human. But it's a good start.

Time to Look Inside

Debra, who worked twenty-four years in big corporate marketing jobs, is taking time off for the first time. Like a typical Type A achiever, she's categorized her priorities so that she'll cover all her bases. "The first thing I did was put my life in quadrants," said

Debra. "There's the personal quadrant, the family quadrant, the community quadrant, the business quadrant. The personal quadrant means I work out with a trainer three days a week and try to go on the treadmill. I've made ten doctor's appointments that I haven't done, deferred maintenance in a sense. I realized that you just keep going until something really needs to get fixed."

(Debra, who's still in her time off, later reported to me that she'd lost twenty pounds in just a few months and reduced her blood pressure significantly. "And I sleep at night," she said with a smile.)

"There's the family piece," she continued. "My three children are at fabulous ages. You have no idea how much you've missed when you don't see the day-to-day stuff. We have breakfast together, I drive them to the bus or to school. And there's the time with my husband."

She admitted how her time with her husband seemed to fall in line after the kids, her mother, and the job. "He was able to fend for himself and that's not fair, either. For the community part, now I'm a class parent for my son's class. I'm getting involved with the education foundation."

She's using this time to explore what she wants to put in her business quadrant. She's been meeting with potential partners—from startups to advisory boards to large corporations. "The realignment of the balance of my life has been the most challenging and rewarding result of the time off so far," says the newly (and somewhat) relaxed Debra.

Once she left her senior job at Sun Microsystems, Lalita outlined her "internal journey." "I tried to find myself. I tried to find the inner child. I did some really bad painting. Burned the canvases. Suddenly, there were all those hours in the week where I wasn't getting a hundred and fifty e-mails, so I ended up doing genealogy, which has been a very off-and-on hobby for years. I traced my family back to the 1400s. I got very involved in the chase. I worked it like a job, because I only had an on-and-off switch, so I sort of flicked it on. And eventually I found the [slave] bill of sale of my great-great-great-grandmother.

"The genealogy led me to write my first book, *Cane River*," she said. "It's a pesky little thing that I didn't know how to write. I had to teach myself. But, you know, if not me, who's going to do it?" (Her pesky talent turned out to be a national best-seller.)

Time to Keep Track

Journals are another way of keeping track of your inner time off. When I took my leave, I started a journal for the first time. I never thought I would have the patience to write each night, and feared that I was setting myself up for more "work" or more guilt if I didn't keep it up. I discovered something totally different.

The journal became my way of expressing my feelings throughout the time off. Some women tell me that they never flip back and reread what they wrote, but by doing so I could observe the tremendous changes in myself. I met other women who found that writing and visualizing what they were feeling was a way to untangle long-buried feelings. You might use the questions at the end of these chapters to get you started.

"Basically, I used that first year really to discover me again," said Donna D. "I did a lot of journaling. I pulled it out the other day and I was reading some of it, and it sort of shocked me. I was thinking, God, did I really feel that bad? That I was putting that kind of thing down on paper was eerie for me."

Donna D. also created a collage as a tool to clarify her time-off thinking. "I picked out words and pictures that were meaningful to me: 'Communities. Spirit. The millennium. The go-getter. Freedom to think. The pathfinder. Ahh. Entrepreneurial excellence. Once upon a time. Intelligence. Can you survive this? The network effect.' I made a big bulletin board. I look at it every day because I just want to be reminded of what I went through to get where I am."

When Lisa K. was home recovering from her mastectomy, she started a journal rather than obsess about her job as she healed. "It took me eight weeks before I could really walk again, so I sat in my chair in front of the TV with my books and my journal. I wrote and thought and I wrote and I took painkillers. I really just went inward and I made a decision that something had to change. That's where it began, this soul searching of, what is my life about?"

Time to Get Physical

Drop the image of a woman goofing off in a La-Z-Boy recliner. While these women were "on," they rarely had time to sleep, let alone exercise. But time off unleashes physical energy and new willpower to reenergize office chair–ridden bodies.

Once I was free of my packed calendar, I couldn't stop moving. Dancing, kickboxing, ice-skating, yoga, gardening. Even on those few days when I'd start to worry about what would come next, I'd put on my sneakers and walk out the door to get some oxygen and energy back. I wasn't alone. Nearly every woman told me that they reinstituted their exercise routine to feel strong again . . . inside and out.

Lalita was able to track her descent into burnout by watching the decline in her racquetball game over the years. Once off, she applied her Type A patterns to her newfound workout resolve. Lalita laughed, "Actually, I went way overboard for quite a long time. I was exercising anywhere from twelve to twenty hours a week. I needed to do that to reclaim some of what I had had before. I lost forty pounds."

Donna D. found her own outlet. "I walk nine holes on the golf course and ride nine holes. Now I'm bicycling, too. The exercise was key."

Eileen, who spent much of her year off helping her husband through his cancer treatments, found relief in working out. "I know what an antidepressant exercise can be. I lost a lot of weight. I worked out about three days a week and got in great shape." I'm not pushing time off as a weight-loss technique, but it worked for dozens of women I've interviewed. While work can be an excuse not to exercise, the real culprit is our overtaxed minds, which lists exercise as just another chore.

If a leg up on career advancement motivates you to take time to exercise, realize that companies link physical energy and success. As a spokesperson from Charles Schwab said, "We're looking for energy and creativity. It's hard to be like that without rejuvenating."[6]

Time to Rest

The flip side of the exercise coin is rest. When Liz took her first time off in the summer, she managed to get some rest, as well as get moving. "I decided that my goal was to not leave the state of Oregon for the entire two months, that I just wanted to stay home. I wanted to wake up in my own bed every single morning. I slept late every morning, since I had a ten-year sleep deficit. I'd take a nap every afternoon. I really did nothing. It was fantastic."

Years and years of running on empty can almost convince you that sleep isn't necessary. One of the earliest pleasures of time off is the sensation of letting your body fall into its natural rhythms. Sleeping when you want to, putting your feet up just to take it easy, ignoring the alarm clock, and listening to your own breathing and daylight to tell you when to wake up. Some women were amazed at just how tired their bodies were once they let go.

I've always been a fan of spas, especially those where women can stay overnight for a time. While the aura of a spa may seem more about faces slathered in mud packs, the truth is that today's spas are deeply involved in helping women revive and explore their inner spirits and focus on wellness. I've heard stories of women who actually cry on the massage table, because they are so in need of gentle touch, rest, and empathy. Though a destination spa might seem costly, you may discover that, rather than spend your travel money vegging on a beach, a spa vacation might be just what the doctor ordered. Meditation, yoga, tai chi, and just swinging in a hammock are relaxation aids you can take home with you.

Our brains need a rest, too. In a study from *Take Back Your Time*, Joe Robinson reports that "continuous time on a task causes us to get overtasked. CAT scans of fatigued brains look exactly like those that are sound asleep."[7] Your exhausted brain knows when to shut down, even if you won't let it.

As you plan your time off, plan naps and early nights as part of your recovery from overcommitting to your job. The afternoon siesta or the late-morning wake-up is as therapeutic as the workout sessions that fill a vacationing Type A's dance card.

Deb is still in the middle of her time off, and fluctuates between enjoying the time and racing to potential job interviews. "I'm trying not to feel compelled to work at that frantic pace, but what I haven't gotten good at yet is sitting and doing nothing." That's the workaholic's definition of rest.

Try to resist your impulse to use your time to catch up on chores and errands. In a 2004 survey conducted by Just Ask a Woman and research firm TNS on behalf of Starcom media and Yahoo, women were asked what they would do with an extra hour in each day. Although women claimed to desire time with family and friends, they admitted that they'd actually probably use the spare time to do errands and chores, like laundry. The habitual "to-dos" are more deeply ingrained than our ability "to be." It's okay to get some things organized to clear your space and your mind, but realize that those little appointments can become a big-time sinkhole. Set aside some time for nothing, too.

Time to Move On

Sometimes a permanent move to an entirely new change of scene is spurred by time off. The most idyllic story I heard about how geography influenced time off belongs to Ardith. Here's her typical day in her dream location in Santa Fe.

"I get up, take a mile-and-a-half walk with my dog, Cleo, a black Lab," says Ardith. "Then I have a healthy breakfast and check the computer, because I am working on a couple of marketing projects. I keep the afternoon open. I exercise every day. I read a book in the afternoon. I make a full, healthy dinner. Different parts of my brain are getting stimulation—family time, creative time, fitness time.

"I always loved arts and music. I sang as a kid, but was too practical to pursue it. Now I'm advertising for a guitarist to accompany me, so I can do the lounge circuit in Santa Fe. I'm taking classes in beaded jewelry–making. Also, I am on the marketing committee for the Georgia O'Keeffe Museum."

While her list of activities might seem pretty active for someone taking a break, the truth is that these are all things that Ardith loves. Type A good girls aren't afraid of being busy. They'd just rather be busy following their passions, rather than their Palm Pilots.

Friends are now part of her daily life. "I get time to socialize and entertain. In the working years, I stopped doing that. I used to think, When am I going to clean? When can I shop? I love meeting other women who have time to have lunch. We talk about things that aren't market share."

If that isn't an ad for the value of taking time off, I don't know what is.

Time to Be Clear

Taking time off is a slow awakening. It's like taking a long mental shower, where your mind relaxes enough to have an outpouring of fresh inspiration. Once you relax, ideas flourish. Clarity comes. Time off helps us douse the crazy notions we build up about perfection and pleasing. With the space of time and your nose off the grindstone, it's so much easier to see what you might become. You just need to learn to let this awakening arrive at its own pace.

Patience is a challenge for Type As who are used to immediate results. Time off helps you get comfortable with ambivalence, allowing yourself to be "out there" without a plan and being open to what you don't even realize is coming your way. Several women told me, "You just put yourself out there, and things happen." What a difference from the nine-to-five to-do list that we grew up on.

Letting go means giving up the control and determination to win that plague Type As. It means not trying to hurry to do every single thing right, as good girls do. Lalita summed it up this way: "My big lesson was about letting go and understanding that I didn't have control. As a matter of fact, if I did, I was clenching it too tightly."

I asked her how someone who knew her would compare her to her pre-leave self. "They would say I was a lot looser," she said. "And that I didn't have to be in charge nearly as much. I don't have to be purposeful every minute of the day anymore. And I don't want to be."

Lalita says she's traded her sharpness for insight and perspective. She's gained enough time to actually be able to sit back and evaluate options. How does her new life compare to her former one? "My job was about manipulating on a constant basis. Now I can let things wash over. My name is Lalita. But a man who used to be my head of engineering actually said to me recently, 'You know, I always knew there was a "Lita" in there somewhere.' " Lalita smiled at this revelation of the "real her."

Dr. Kaye Moore agrees that the value of time off is the time to reconnect with who you really are. "When you know who you are, and you value yourself, you're clear on what you feel and think, you radiate like a beacon and people are attracted to that." Even if women return to their same job after time off, if they've been able to develop a hobby or an avocation or a new area of study, they can become more multidimensional women instead of a one-track, work-centered woman.

Time to Take Your Own Time Off

When you're ready to rest, time off provides the space to evaluate what's important and to refresh yourself for the next part of your life. Is a break without risks? No. Without some bruises to your ego? No. But taking time off comes with this promise: In the space of unscheduled time, you are likely to discover who you are and what matters to you.

Whether you take off a week or a month or a year, make it long enough for you to achieve your goals of assessment or rest, of volunteering or spending more family time, or developing a new skill or a new set of coping behaviors for when you return. Cut yourself off from work, as hard as that is. Do not continue any weekly conference calls. Do not check e-mail; in fact, if you are truly addicted, you might want to ask that your account be temporarily shut down while you are gone so you're not tempted.

Some experts say that maintaining a light level of contact, such as reading up on your industry or touching base with your office off and on throughout your leave, is a good way to smooth reentry and stay on top of your management, especially if you are on a company-sponsored leave. My caution to the good girls is to be careful that you don't slip back into caring more about your colleagues' progress than your own. Before you know it, your time off will turn into a satellite version of your office.

Personally, I found that it was important not to fraternize with my friends from work. As much as several of them were girlfriends as well as colleagues, the glue of our relationship was the job. It's fun, but insidious and filled with the gossip, the complaints, and the daily ups and downs. Don't leave work and then let work come to visit you. This is your time, not theirs.

Be sure to keep your calendar as blank as you can, but dot it with some things that give you purpose and propulsion. For instance, I found that just seeing a notation on my calendar for a lunch with a girlfriend on Wednesday and a dance lesson on Monday night gave me the structure that I needed. Going cold turkey from twelve-hour days may be too traumatic and, in fact, make you feel uneasy.

Build in a combination of things that give you mental, physical, and spiritual stimulation. Include the people you love in big doses, as long as you don't overadopt their agendas as your own or make them feel like a check mark on your to-do list. Experiment with things you've never done as a way to awaken your senses and talents.

Lessons from Time Off: Joan's Story

Earlier in the book, I described Joan as the high-level fashion marketing executive who decided to take a year off in Paris. She quit her job with its Million-Dollar Mondays, met with a financial advisor, enrolled her child in a Paris school, and rented an apartment with her husband in the city of her dreams.

From her early years, Joan had one characteristic that was different than other good girls. Even though she was a high achiever, she knew how to decide when an A mattered and when it didn't. "I breezed through high school but when I went to college, I had a hard time. I worked at the subjects I liked, but those I didn't like, I thought, I'll get a C and I don't care."

She described herself as a "focused kid," and that focus propelled her through her career. When she found herself losing focus on those long Monday meetings, she saw it as an early indicator that something was wrong. Her life looked glamorous on the outside, but was hectic inside. "Life was getting overwhelming," said Joan. "My husband was commuting and living in Chicago. My daughter was in adolescence. I was on the road traveling constantly. The politics at my company were getting really haywire." She started daydreaming about retirement and cashing out, even though she was only in her late forties.

She called a time out. Joan said, "The best thing I did was take the time off at an age when I could appreciate it and understand it. I was forty-eight. I think there is something important about being in your forties because you've had all this time to figure out what wrongs you want to right or what you desire or what's the piece of you that's bubbling to get out."

She chose Paris because her fashion trips had given her the taste, but never the time to enjoy it. "I knew that Paris would refuel me. There is something very calming to me about Paris. It was food for the soul, this city that I loved. I was very drawn to it."

Even though Joan was looking for relief from her own over-worked life, she realized that the trip could be a great way to bring her and her family together while there was still time to enjoy each other. "My husband said if we go now, as opposed to at the end of our lives, it would truly affect how we go forward."

I wondered what Joan's thirteen-year-old daughter's reaction to leaving her friends and moving time zones away for a year was. "She said, 'You're not kidding me, are you, Mom?' And I said, 'No.' She was so happy. We got there in August, we left just this past September, and she is completely fluent. She really, really loved it. We all fell in love with the way of life over there." The desire to raise their daughter in the U.S. and their own careers and financial needs were the factors that brought them home.

When we work every day with the same people, who eventually pick up the same language of work, the same worries and complaints, we don't even realize how narrow our world can become. By living in a completely different environment, Joan learned the joy of being with people with an entirely different worldview. "My cooking class was really a great thing for me. Even though it was taught in English, it included women from all over the world."

Paris became so much more than art and fashion and food and history. Paris became the place she fell even more deeply in love with her daughter.

Her years as a manic worker hadn't left room for some of the simplest pleasures of being a mom. "The hardest thing for me to get used to was that I could be home when my daughter came home from school. I didn't know to do that. Isn't that bizarre? I had never been home when she came home from school. I'd be out exploring, and suddenly I'd look at my watch and say, 'Maybe I should be home when Hannah gets home.' It just shows how far gone I was."

Until we get significant time away, we lose track of just how abnormal an overworked life is. And unfortunately, no matter how much we love them, we expect our families to be good sports when it comes to allowing us even more time to work harder. Or we expect them to assume the same guilt and drive as we have for our work.

Imagine the contrast Joan felt each afternoon. She was amazed at how much more she learned about Hannah's life just by being there to listen at the end of her school days. "I would have a cup of tea in the kitchen when she would arrive home. Hannah would sit at the table and all the stuff would come out. As a result, we have a wonderful relationship. We always had a good one, but I think she probably had a lot of stress. I didn't realize how my stress affected her, but it did."

An article in *The Wall Street Journal* warned about the legacy effect of workaholic parents infecting their children.[8] If children only see their parents heading to work because they "have to," they don't develop their own healthy attitudes toward the joys of the job.

She and her daughter have an even more open and caring partnership than before. "A couple weeks ago, she said to me, 'Joan the mom is much nicer than Joan the executive vice president,' which was perfect timing on her part, because I was right in the middle of interviewing again. It's just a reminder I am never going to go back to the way I was."

As a going-away present at the end of their sojourn, Hannah gave Joan a book about calmness. She wrote this inscription, "Mom, may you always remember the limp-wristed time in Paris." Joan explained, "I always joke about how relaxed she is. I do this test with Hannah where I ask her to put her hand up and then I push against the topside of her hand and her hand collapses forward easily. It practically falls off the end of her wrist. She used to do the test on my wrist, and it was like my wrist was made out of concrete. But when we were winding down, she said, 'Give me your wrist!' and she pushed and it was really floppy."

Joan still uses that wrist test to see if she's keeping her promise. She wants to return to a marketing job in New York City, which can test her "calm quotient" to the max. But she feels that her time off has changed her.

"I'm anxious to go to work and try out my new skills. I believe I will approach my job very differently. I think I have stronger resolve than I've had before. Now I really know the people I have to please are me and my family. It's not about what makes somebody else happy.

"Work will only get so much of me," said Joan. "It won't get my heart and soul anymore. Now, when things go wrong, I ask, Will it affect the quality of my life? Is it a priority? Is it not a priority? My husband laughs because I'm always saying, 'It really doesn't matter.' I say that a lot now."

YOUR TURN

If you gave yourself permission to rest, what would you do with:

One hour a day to yourself? ————————————————

————————————————————————————————

One week off? ——————————————————————

————————————————————————————————

————————————————————————————————

One month? ————————————————————————

————————————————————————————————

————————————————————————————————

One year? ——————————————————————————

————————————————————————————————

————————————————————————————————

————————————————————————————————

————————————————————————————————

The rest of your life? ——————————————————

————————————————————————————————

————————————————————————————————

————————————————————————————————

————————————————————————————————

If you could travel on your time off, where would you go? ——

————————————————————————————————

————————————————————————————————

Make a list of love to-dos, like exercise or learn a language or volunteer to help a favorite cause. ————————————————

————————————————————————————————

What about the journey inside? Write as if you were filling in the first page of your journal on your first day off. How do you feel? What will you do?

_____

_____

_____

_____

Name the friends you'd like to spend time with. _____

_____

How's your love life? Could time off make a difference there?

_____

_____

_____

CHAPTER SEVEN

Time After Time Off

There's a commonly held belief that once they get out of the rat race, women will never get back on the track again. But that theory underestimates what makes Type A good girls tick. In fact, nearly all the women in this book returned to work.

This is supported by a 2002 Catalyst study of follow-up interviews with women who left their jobs. Marcia Brumit Kropf, then vice president for research and information services, said, "Often what we find is myth-breaking. For example, many women say they are leaving the company to spend time with their families, but one year later they are working someplace else."[1]

Indeed, we know that the vast majority of women do work and that belies some of the popular media coverage that women are opting out of work for long periods of time. A cover story in *Time* magazine explains: "What some experts are zeroing in on is the first-ever drop-off in workplace participation by married mothers with a child less than one year old. That figure fell from 59 percent in 1997 to 53 percent in 2002 ... and the figure was roughly the same in 2000. ... Significantly, the drop was mostly among women who were white, over thirty, and well educated."[2] The two "Karens" in this book fall into that category.

But even those who may have taken some time off to be with

children in the very early years return to the workforce in large numbers. Whether they are sequencing by alternating between work and childcare, or stopping out for a time, or just walking out for a break from burnout, I found that, after time off, most women eventually return to work.

Hard work defines and excites us. Our "get it done" gumption is alive and well after a break. With a little breathing space, our energy kicks up and we return refreshed to our jobs, or we replace our former jobs with more satisfying ones.

Some rejoin their companies, some join new ones, some start their own ventures, some seek a change of scenery or lifestyle, but all rechannel their talents and ambitions to align with their passions.

When women return to their jobs after a company-sponsored sabbatical, their loyalty and enthusiasm returns with them. Candice Lange, director of Workforce Partnering for Eli Lilly and Company, says that returning women are happier because they've met the need that caused them to take time off. "They come back ready to be recharged and ready to go on with their careers."

So what happened to the women in this book when they returned to "normal life"? Their "ever after" stories are as different as they are. As you hear the stories of how these women moved forward, you'll see the after effect of their time off in their changed attitudes. They discovered how to apply their good girl drive differently, and how to be more selective about who deserves their one hundred percent attention. They learned to draw the line between overworking and underliving. They discovered their true callings, and assessed whether their current careers were still able to satisfy the person they'd grown to become. They resurrected long-buried talents or channeled their prior work experience into totally new avenues. Most finally created space in their lives for their relationships, as well as for their responsibilities.

All agreed that the best part of time off isn't being off. The real benefit was discovering who and what they became after. The women I interviewed didn't dwell on tales of the trip around the world or the mornings of sleeping late. Their revelations focused on how time off changed their outlooks and even their work choices. Simply said, returning from a break is like restarting your life.

Going Home Again

Julie, who traveled to the Far East for a year, returned to her same firm in Washington, D.C., with a different position and a fresh point of view. "Before I left, what I did every day defined me," she said. "I've learned my worth is more than nine to five and that definitely came from taking time off and getting a wider perspective. I realize that I don't always have to be the one that saves the day. I don't have to be the good girl all the time. Still, I find it a surprise every day that I wake up happy. I keep waiting for the other shoe to drop."

After her year at home with Kate, Jane C. is back teaching in her high school. She laughs when she realizes that one of her goals during her time off was to clean the front hall closet. "That closet still isn't clean and nobody died because of it. My house was messier the year I took off and the clothes didn't get washed as often. I was busy living life. I realized it was okay to breathe." That "let it go" attitude has stayed with her.

One of the differences she notices in herself is her tolerance for lateness. As a teacher, she was always a stickler for assignments being turned in on time. Now when a student is delinquent with a paper and has a good reason, like a family event or attending his sister's soccer game, she's more patient. It's not that she's dropped her standards. It's just that she measures what's important differently.

Her advice if you're fearful of taking a leave? "It may seem scary at first, but that's because for most women not working is the unknown. The unknown is always scary."

Barbara, who's married, a mom, and a telecommuting literary publicist in Austin, Texas, agrees with Jane C. that women just don't know what it's like not to work hard. "Women flat out don't give themselves permission to ever be off-duty, yet we're the most productive members of society you'll find," she said. "We need to give ourselves permission to take a break. Everyone will benefit from our refreshed attitudes and ability to tackle our multitasking head on."

Creating Work You Love

Not everyone returned to their former jobs by choice. After she finished her therapy for her mastectomy, Lisa K. had to return to her marketing job in order to save enough money to afford her dream of moving with her husband to Vermont. She kept a piece of slate from the Vermont property on her desk as a talisman to get her through what was still a manic work environment. That little piece of stone kept her focused on her bigger goal, and kept her from slipping back into stressed work habits. After two years, she was able to make the move to the country.

Her life is now dramatically changed from the intensity of Manhattan. "We just stripped away so much of the noise. Now I can listen more, especially to my own intuition."

Her beauty and health products business continues to grow. "We are getting ready to expand our Gem Therapy Skin Care line and this fall we will be giving away samples of Topaz Foot Butter (topaz represents personal strength and power) to all the [cancer] survivors in the Race for the Cure in Boston," says Lisa K., her passion clearly showing. "We are also setting up a foundation to support alternative treatments and screening for women's cancers. Our thermal imaging business for the earlier detection of breast cancer is taking off and our products will be in distribution at Bloomingdale's, JCPenney, Bed Bath & Beyond, and several other smaller department stores."

"Most importantly," she said, "I'm coming up on my five-year anniversary of being cancer free this fall and have been very healthy."

Thanks to time off, Lisa K. realized that she could finally let go of letting others define her goals. "Before I was listening to my projection of what I thought my parents' voice was. I grew up thinking I could be my mom and my dad. My dad runs a company. My mom was a stay-at-home mom. I could be both," she laughed. "I could have it all. Now I've redefined what 'all' is."

Taking action on your beliefs is a way to create work you love. While in Cape May for her week-long, solo birthday celebration, Monique made the decision to relinquish her role as the editor-in-chief of *Essence* and devote herself to growing her bed-and-breakfast business. While at the shore, she put a bid in on a second bed-and-breakfast to add a seashore property to her existing Brooklyn inn. Though her real estate decision was quick, she's taken the last couple of years to develop a new approach to simplifying her "time on."

She laughingly describes her new no-frills uniform. After years of wearing heels and makeup and great hair, each day she suits up in a black sweatshirt and black jeans. So do all the employees of her Akwaaba House. She says, "The uniform is not just for them, it's to make life simpler for me."

Since her leave, Donna D. moved from a corporate HR job to individual counseling. "I signed up for Coach U. and I started the coaching practice, helping people one-on-one. My mantra for my life continues to be the line from the Robert Frost poem about the road less traveled. It's not always an easy road, but I'm glad I've taken it and the time off really helped. As I look back, I would do it again because that voluntary severance from my company was truly a gift—the opportunity to reconnect with my husband and son and even my mom and dad and brother and sister."

Liz converted her marketing and communication skills into something she cared about—reaching other women by connecting with her own sisters. Together with her four sisters, she founded *The Satellite Sisters*, a syndicated radio talk show, as well as a website. They also wrote a book together, called *Satellite Sisters' Uncommon Senses*. All of her activities come under the mantle of her personal mission, she calls the Four Fs: "fun, friends, family, and philanthropy." Most refreshing is her outlook now as an experimenter, really a pioneer, into new ways of working that go beyond the good girl mantra of pleasing. "I don't think about success or failure anymore. I try new things and I am very satisfied when they work, but if they don't, there's no shame in just moving on to the next idea."

Finding Out Who You Really Are

As we zip along the fast track of our lives and careers, we can move so fast that we lose sight of who we are. After time off, many women rediscovered the person they had grown up to be.

Jane C. put it this way: "I learned a lot about myself. I learned that I love being a mom. I love being married to Tony. I stopped worrying as much about what people thought of me. I started going to church on a regular basis and I liked it."

Being off also helped Jane realize how much she wanted to return to her teaching position. "Taking time away made me see how much it really meant to me, besides the paycheck. I am more positive about my work and my home and how they are intertwined.

"I learned that I have choices . . . lots of them," Jane concluded. "I strongly believe that taking the year off has made me a better person. It was the smartest thing I've ever done. Besides marrying Tony, that is."

Karen N.'s pajama business, inspired when she started her leave and spent her days in her husband's pajamas and oversize T-shirts, grew exponentially. She began with the help of one person sewing up samples in her kitchen. Now she's got 125 people in her company and distribution in major retailers like Nordstrom for a brand that's loved by women around the country.

But her priorities as a mom remains solid. "Family commitments went on the calendar first, like anniversaries, birthdays, proms, finals, as my daughter grew up and got busier. I've kept home life number one."

For Karen N., work life and personal life are integrated rather than competing on opposite ends of a work/life seesaw. "Compartmentalizing and separating my home life and work life simply didn't work for me. I found success by integrating my passion through all elements of my life."

She realized that the idea of "comfort," not just in soft pjs and wraps, but emotional comfort, could become a guiding theme for her life. "My passion for comfort crosses all boundaries in my life, from the personal to the professional, from family to friends, from work to community," said Karen N. "By embracing this, I have been able to come full circle as a woman."

Putting Your Good Girl to Work

When Eileen left her job in magazine publishing, I happened to be heading New York Women in Communications, and I was looking for someone to fill the vacant presidency of our scholarship foundation. I asked Eileen to take it on. Her year off spent volunteering at the foundation helped qualify her to become executive director of the American Montessori Society. For Eileen, it was like coming home again, since she had started out her career twenty years before as a teacher.

Diane switched out of her corporate PR job to head a cancer support organization. Diane said, "I wanted to take my skills and do something more rewarding. I actually had planned to teach and had signed up for four courses. I thought I'd go on some nonprofit boards and do a little consulting, which someone told me was called a portfolio career. But then the job of managing a nonprofit cancer support organization came along, and having lost a sister to cancer, it just seemed like the right thing to do."

Women who accepted jobs in the nonprofit sector traded some

of their former financial compensation for the emotional satisfaction of doing a job they love. For some, their lifelong savings will bridge the gap during their later career years. Others accept that they are spending a few years doing something that matters. Whether they will return to more lucrative jobs over time is not yet known. Most assert they would not return to jobs that sapped their energy and passion.

Ardith acknowledged the satisfaction of doing pro-bono work after a corporate career. "I've been helping several organizations in Santa Fe develop marketing plans. Most of these nonprofits really don't have people with the same skill sets that are developed in major corporations. I really feel that I am contributing something that they would never be able to do on their own and helping them so much, and that's been a great feeling."

As Time Goes By

The benefits of taking time off continue to unfold long after the time off ends. At first, the changes you make in your life may seem odd to others, especially if you create something off the beaten track. But with time, you can discover that there really are completely new ways to work and live.

When I first interviewed former trial lawyer Kay, she was reluctant to go public about the knitting website she had created with a friend, "because people make fun of me for it." Since then, their "two-headed blog" has exploded into a site frequented by thousands of women who write in. "Doing the blog provides an opportunity to continue to do two of the things I liked most about the working life: to write, and mentor people," said a highly energized Kay. "We have created a microcommunity on the Internet. The more I find out about these women's lives, the more I feel that what we are doing is worthwhile."

Kerry was another woman who was wary of talking about the venture she started following her high-flying public relations career.

She was matter-of-fact and low-key with me as she explained that she was making "fake boobs"—it's an "accessory business," she said.

Now, with her wearable silicone breast enhancers and accessories dubbed "the Better Boob Job," she's built a burgeoning enterprise. "If it wasn't for the time off, I wouldn't have been able to start my own business or grow it to what it is today. My product is now in three hundred clothing boutiques, I've been on the *Today* show and in *InStyle* magazine. I would do it again!"

Watching women go from their first tenuous time-off steps to full-blown euphoria taught me that time off just gets better with time.

Still Searching

Emerging from time off with a fabulous new plan doesn't happen for everyone. In fact, I've been told that my own five-week turnaround may set up impossible expectations for other women. But my new life didn't happen overnight.

Along with my colleagues, I had experimented with new techniques for listening to women as part of pitching new business for the agency. And even though I emerged from my leave with a business concept, it took several months just to get it going. Finding the perfect blend of living a happy life, as well as a successful, professional one, will be an ongoing challenge to my still intense Type A tendencies.

Some of the women I met are still in transition, like Lisa B., who has moved to Florida since her leave, and is experimenting with real estate investing and travel consulting, which actually bring in more income than the corporate travel job she quit. Her path is still riddled with doubts and detours, sorting out what she wants and what she doesn't. "I learned that you have to be willing to 'give it up,' " she said. "The more pressure I put on myself to have the answers, the more I felt confused and further from finding my path. Sometimes I wonder what it would be like to go back to corporate

America. Would my perspective be different? Could I prevent myself from slipping back into the grind? I don't know, but I do know that it feels great not to have submitted a vacation request in over a year!"

Joan is still looking for the right job after her year in Paris, but even without a definite plan, she doesn't regret leaving her big retailing job for her year abroad with her family. "I would most definitely do it again and highly recommend it. One of my greatest lessons was to focus on 'what matters' and, in the end, not a lot really matters. That realization has freed me up and I find I am happier, more relaxed, and clearer about what I want for myself and for my family. That year was a precious gift that I gave to myself. It was meant to be life changing and I will stay vigilant that it remains so."

At the start of my conversations with Ann, she was elated with her plan to take five weeks of endorsed freedom from her editorial job to rest and develop the concept for a book and documentary about the first generation of children with Down syndrome who had been mainstreamed.

But just before she was to start her time off, her plans collapsed. "Those weeks that I was 'preparing' for my leave were, to be honest, miserable," confessed Ann. "I was working 48/7 and had no idea that I was hitting a wall. My boss was unhappy with my editing. No one got any Christmas presents until weeks after the fact. I couldn't sleep. And all just to take a sabbatical to prove that I was in control of my destiny. I realized that what I really wanted wasn't to run off and do this project. I just wanted to know that the hours and hours of work I was putting in to be there for my company, for my family, for everyone but me was worth it. I decided to delay my sabbatical."

I admit that I felt disappointed on Ann's behalf. Why couldn't she get the break she deserved? But Ann's attitude was more realistic. "The reality is that I could not just walk away and do what I wanted," she said. "I pay the bills and without my job, I wouldn't be able to do much. So I am working with what I have, and finding small ways to do what I want for me. I am doing some of the best editing I have ever done. I started exercising. I connected with a woman at my firm who had just come back from a leave and we meet each week to talk. I feel more focused and optimistic and I also know my time for more of me will come."

Just conceiving the plan for time off forced Ann to face herself in the mirror. She didn't take the time, but she did take steps to start to rebalance her life.

For once in your life, it's okay not to have everything figured out immediately. Isa started her dance studio with only a belief in herself. "I believe that you can create your own reality. I am certainly building something out of nothing. There's no official report on what the fire dancing business is going to do. I am the report, believing that I will figure it out as I go."

Monique has this perspective: "I think what's important is understanding that having a rich life has a lot more to do with being content with who you are and what difference you make in the world than how big your paycheck is." That's something that time off can teach you in spades.

Prepare for Reentry

Even though you may have spent your time off trekking a mountain or studying Greek, the work world continues on at its breakneck speed. The trick of successful reentry is your ability to readjust to the pace without losing your newfound perspective. This is not a time to rev up your Type A "hurry up and get back in gear"/"show 'em how it's done" instincts.

Walk, don't run, into the next phase of what you will do. Designate time near the end of your leave to analyze what you've learned, how you've changed, and to set goals for what's next. As your energy resurges, you will find yourself designing the new life you hope to lead.

I purposely waited until the end of my time off to do this self-analysis. I knew that if I made a knee-jerk decision too early in the process, I'd probably rationalize myself right back into my old habits and replicate my overworked schedule. I didn't want to clog up my relaxing time with career concerns until I was operating with calmness and insight. With that perspective, I was able to honestly make my list of "What I love to do and what I'm good at" and "What I hate to do and what I'm bad at." That list gave me the black-and-white truth of what I needed to do to take my next steps.

In her book *I Could Do Anything I Wanted If Only I Knew What It Was*, Barbara Sher has a wonderful exercise called "The Job from Heaven, the Job from Hell."[3] She suggests that you describe, soup to nuts, everything those jobs would entail for you. In your "heavenly" job, where would the office be? Or would you be virtual? What kind of people would you work with? Would you rather work alone? What would your day-to-day duties and rewards be? The "hell" job description is a great way to alert yourself to all the tasks, environments, and toxic behaviors you'll want to avoid.

When I did the "heaven" exercise, I "cast" the sort of people whom I'd work with, and I envisioned how we'd interact, how we'd try to regard each other's need to have a life outside work. I got as specific as the look of the rooms and the color of the walls. Even if it sounded like an impossible nirvana, by being specific, I was able to direct my efforts toward making that happen.

Five years later, Just Ask a Woman is even more than I had hoped for. In fact, I looked back at my copy of Barbara's book and read the notes I'd written in the margins. For the most part, I have actually created a little "heaven" at work. I work with amazing women in an environment that's intense in its work ethic, yet loose in its interactive, free-flowing style. Even the office looks as I imagined. My mix of activities between speaking, writing, and consulting has evolved as I'd hoped. (The exception is that I haven't yet had my weekly appearances in a Broadway show, which I had brazenly put on the list!) That's the magic of time off for a good girl. You can take the time to think of the small details and the big dreams that make you happy.

Part of growing through this process is seeing how you can keep the best of what makes you "you," yet start to ease out the downside of the overly good girl traits and the Type A urgency that everyone else expects. How can you evolve from good to good enough? How can you shift from "right away" to "as soon as I can"? Making big changes starts with baby steps.

Taking Time to Form New Habits

Type As cultivate their workaholic tendencies over a lifetime. Like putting on weight, the pounds slowly get out of control over time, and it can take just as much time to work your way back down the scale. We need to unlearn some deeply ingrained habits (like the reflex to say "yes") and fears (like "who am I without my title?") in order to move forward. Like other recoveries, undoing an overactive work ethic is a process.

Coach Marcia Worthing acknowledges the need to take your time. She says, "You can't go from A to Z. You have to go from A to F to M to whatever. Appreciate that for every step you take forward, you'll probably take one or two back. It's not a straight path out of your old life."

In practice, some of us never lose our Type A instincts. Even though she's moved to the relaxed desert of Santa Fe, Ardith's urge to lead and impatience to succeed are alive and well. "At volunteer places, I find myself wanting to stand up and take the Magic Marker and take over the meeting." Time off isn't a wholesale conversion to Type B behavior; rather, it's a gradual mellowing. (At least she wasn't trying to merge the O'Keeffe Museum into the Met.)

You will need new skills to navigate what might be the same stresses, even if you change jobs. Assume that you'll instinctively still set high goals and seek approval, especially at first. Dr. Redford B. Williams of the Duke University Medical Center advises caution after taking a break. "If you just come back and get right back into the same grind, then the break is not going to do you much good. Before you know it, you'll be back with too many things to do, too-high adrenaline and cortisol levels, and sleep problems will start up again. You need to have some ways of prioritizing what's important. Being able to say "no" more often. Being able to evaluate your emotional reactions when you're under stress. You need relationship skills and listening empathy, to be emotionally competent when you come back from the break."

Practice on the easy things while you're off. Say no to an unimportant invitation, the kind of thing you would have attended out of obligation, rather than desire. Or say "yes" to something that you may have used work as an excuse to get out of, because you were "too busy." Try to enjoy the downtime of just being a guest.

Try drawing boundaries around e-mail checking and voice mails, as in "no logging on after seven P.M." If you haven't already, incorporate daily thought-calming rituals into your first days back, like meditating, or following a book like *The Artist's Way* by Julia Cameron, which urges daily writing. Find some physical release like working out or walking with a friend and make it a nonnegotiable appointment on your yet-to-be-filled-in new agenda. Fill those dates in on specific times over the next few months.

Barbara, forty-two, realized that with all the scheduling she does for her children's piano lessons and athletics, she needed to put her own "lessons" on the calendar, too. At forty-one, she decided to run a triathlon and dedicate it to her father, who died ten days before her fortieth birthday. "So on Tuesday nights and Saturday mornings, Mom has triathlon training," said Barbara. "It's a modest amount of time and I found enormous satisfaction in it. The training is a mental break. It's my late-in-life discovery that if the kids have dance and music, well, Mom has triathlon training." (Notice how Barbara didn't take up Type B jogging.)

If this feels like too much work, realize that you eagerly complete your job "homework." Why not put some of your "good girl" precision into preparing to live your life fully?

Avoiding the Saboteurs

A key step in moving forward is dealing with the reaction of others who might want you back the way you were. Beware the saboteurs, friendly or otherwise, who try to undo your new plans before you can even execute them. Many women talked about not knowing how to answer the curious, the skeptical, and the disinterested people in their lives.

Some women learned that it takes time to feel comfortable with the decision to change their lives. When I first spoke with Kay, she was still feeling uncertain about how she was adapting to life at home with her children. But more recently, I heard a new optimism in her voice. "It is almost three years since I left the ranks of New York attorneys, and I think I am finally comfortable with my life again," she said recently. "I no longer feel compelled to tell people at cocktail parties about what I 'used to do,' to validate myself as a person. Nor, however, do I present myself as a 'housewife' or 'full-time mom' (which all moms are); that still goes against the grain and probably always will."

Kay tells a story about how she handles the curious and the rude. "When asked what I 'do,' I feel completely okay about saying that I have young kids and am enjoying spending time with them and doing my own thing," she said. "I no longer feel that I have to present my credentials to prove that to anyone, which is not to say that when a lawyer starts explaining something about his (it's usually a him!) work in an oversimplified way, I don't quickly let him know, 'I'm a lawyer (so you can stop patronizing, mister).' "

The discomfort with the "cocktail party" question popped up, perhaps more often than party invitations do. Kerry said, "One of my biggest fears after making this transition was, 'What am I going to tell people at cocktail parties?' They would ask and I would say 'nothing' and they would laugh or stare at me. There's nothing to say after that."

Liz faced that same "what are you doing now?" question. A male executive told her, "You have a year until you really have to turn up someplace. After that, people will forget about you." Liz laughed, "I was only a month away from the year and I thought, Really? Another month and I'll become a nonperson? It's obviously not true. Once people accept that you're not coming back in some other powerful corporate role, the chairs change around you. A lot of the people I've seen try to step away end up going back. It's not really about the money. They miss having a structure around them that provides power and influence."

If you are someone who needs structure, direct your planning efforts that way. As serene and idyllic as it might seem, sitting alone in a home office will drive you crazy.

Family members can also throw water on your newfound freedom. If your parents are skeptical of your changes, it's understandable. They lived their lives with the belief that you don't just leave a job. "My family keeps asking us, 'When are you going back to work?'" said Ardith, who's firmly ensconced in the Southwest. "They're a little nervous."

This parental reaction is natural. After all, your parents are likely the ones who raised you to work so hard. You're just exercising a little "civilized" disobedience.

On your return, you may also need to reevaluate the boundaries you draw relative to clients and associates who can be "paying saboteurs." Cindy, who created her own consulting business, decided not to fall into the old trap of saying "yes" to every client opportunity: "I try not to do anything that I'd only do if someone paid me to do it. I take client work that I would do even if they weren't paying me. This helps me fill my life with activities I am passionate about. Doing something I'm not that interested in because someone will pay me for it is a drain on my energy—I avoid it whenever possible!"

Making New Friends

One of the most-often-heard observations about life before time off is that women become disconnected from the people in their lives who matter. So one of the first things that gets delightfully restored into their lives is meaningful human contact.

Connecting with other people, men or women, mentors or friends, provides the kind of reinforcement you'll need to solidify your new life. You'll see that relationships can actually lead to success, rather than steal time from it. If we neglected those relationships during our over-busy careers, it's even more critical to take a different approach to the value of networking the second time around.

Donna D., who worked for twenty years at Procter & Gamble, opened her eyes to the value of expanding her network of friends and colleagues beyond her own "corporate four walls." She said, "I really didn't network outside of my company for twenty years. All of a sudden I was going to women's meetings, HR professional meetings, and connecting with people I'd never connected with before. Sometimes we can forget all the outside resources that can keep creating new friendships and new insights."

Women learn that with the space of a little time, they cultivate a deeper and wider circle of new friends. Debra added, "I have been amazed at how many smart, well-educated, hardworking, and creative women I have met who for many different reasons are no longer in full-time careers—or any paying jobs at all. I feel very welcomed by them as I navigate this new territory and the bonds of shared experiences are quite powerful. Also, the reasons women make their choices may appear obvious, but many times there are other underlying issues for an individual's personal choice. These women are the engine that keeps many of these communities going and thriving as they apply skills in a different way."

Personal cheerleaders are important after a break. "Sometimes we don't have cheerleaders in our lives," says Monique. "It's important to surround yourself with people who are going to believe in you even when you don't, who can remind you of your greatness at the times that you're feeling weak."

That also means barring the bad guys from your new life. In my own case, I realize that I've developed an allergy to negative people ever since my leave. I do everything I can to avoid them. Whenever possible, I don't take them on as clients, I don't hire them, and I certainly don't add them to my social life. If all this sounds calculating, it is. A life that is integrated and happy is not an accident. It takes planning, and even discipline, to take the leave and to stay the course afterward.

One of the hardest changes Julie made when she came home was to end a friendship gone stale. In her words, she "broke up with her best friend of twenty years. I'm not sorry about it, because it's one of those relationships that you stay in even when it's not healthy. After all those years of trying to please people and make sure everything was okay, it was a major step for me to realize that I don't have to please everybody."

You can also pay a professional "friend" to help you. Isa hired a life coach. "This is saying, 'I value myself enough to sit down and spend my time, my energy, and my resources on the only thing I am going to have every single day of my life, which is me.' " Patti Clark, a life coach herself, has her own mentors. "I looked for people to help me. You can't do it alone."

Deborah Holmes, the Americas director of the Center for the New Workforce at Ernst & Young, also suggests that you create your own "board of directors." You might include your mother, your best friend, or professional colleagues who really know you. Assembling the board is one thing, listening to their advice is a new step for a Type A woman. Deborah mentions, "One of the questions I like to ask is, 'What do the people who love you most think about your job?' Because you can fool yourself, but you can't fool the people who love you most."

Listen and make adjustments as you proceed in your post–time off endeavors.

Writing It Down

As you think about what you want your post–time off life to be, be willing to commit thoughts to paper. As someone who's used to being "buttoned-up," you might find it particularly disconcerting to feel like you don't know what you ought to be doing. Take a cue from the women in this book, and start with what you love. Don't be literal, like, "I enjoy arguing my point in big meetings." Think conceptually about the nature and content of what makes you happy. "Think about what really gives you satisfaction day to day," says Liz. "I knew that what I loved most about my job was meeting all of those interesting people at Nike. Our radio show, *Satellite Sisters,* still allows me to do that, even though it's a very different thing."

Like Liz, Donna D. recommended building a plan that starts with your own desires and goals. "Begin to think about what you want in your life. When I worked with organizations, I used to help them write a mission for themselves. I'd never done it for myself. I just started putting things down on paper, because when I put them on paper, they're more real."

I agree with Donna wholeheartedly. I pushed myself to come up with a statement that would capture what I wanted to do and to be. One night, I took out a pen and scribbled this on a paper napkin: "To be the most compelling interpreter of women's voices in the marketplace." Then, I crossed out "marketplace" and wrote "world." (Yes, "most" and "world" show that my Type A achievement instincts were still alive.) Those words spelled out a presumptuous mission, but it's what I wanted to shoot for. Alongside that, I wrote the list of everyday living changes I wanted to keep from my time off.

By writing down the core of what you want, you will have a guide to help you decide what you'll say "yes"—and "no"—to in your new life. For instance, under "yes," I would write "exercise, spend time with family, maximum of two nights out during the workweek, vacations without e-mail." Under "no," I'd list "agreeing to work events on weekends, fattening food, taking on a mismatched client just for the money." At the end of this chapter, you'll find a calendar to articulate your own mission.

One Day at a Time

Near the end of my time off, my friend Barrie suggested that I create a prototype calendar of the "perfect week." What would I do each day? Where would I be? Who would I be with? It's a great way to allot time to priorities and to get practical about what it takes to do what you love. See the exercise at the end of this chapter. Put in everything from time with family and friends to working out to resting to creating, whatever. You'll get a picture of what your ideal life might look like.

Of course, there is no perfect planning tool to anticipate all the unknowns of a new life, nor is there a pat system for putting your Type A good girl to bed.

How does a Type A good girl ever redefine life in anything less than 100 percent terms? My friend Diane commented on the nature of women to overestimate just how much they're responsible for. "I'm still Type A but in a different way. My range of passion is different. Whereas everything used to be on one side of the bell curve, now there's more in the middle. Not every single thing is important. I have a '98 percent' theory. A really competent person will spend X amount of time and X amount of money to complete a job 98 percent. But being the Type A perfectionist, they'll say 98 percent isn't good enough. So they spend the same amount of time and money, getting to 99 or 100 percent. That's a waste. Learn to stop at 98."

A friend of mine said, "If Michelangelo were still alive, he'd probably still be touching up the ceiling of the Sistine Chapel." We need to draw boundaries, whether they are lines of time or place, that we call "good enough." Just remembering that our "good enough" is probably far beyond the acceptable norm might be a reassurance. The many other things we can enjoy when we accept "good enough" standards make it worthwhile.

After her time off, Courtney picked small good girl behaviors to let go of first. "I decided to stop hating carbs," she said with a straight face. If she's not happy with what she ordered for breakfast, back it goes. Simple things, but it's the beginning of not saying "yes" when you mean "no."

I still have a hard time saying no and letting go. A funny thing my mom taught me growing up was that I could always say "yes" and then say "no" later. I guess she knew that I had a hard time saying no because I hated disappointing people. But that "out" gave me permission to avoid the grown-up "nos" that I needed to learn to say. Over the last couple of years, I've practiced saying "no" on the easy things, like, "Can you participate in this conference call at seven A.M.?" or, "Can you do me a favor for the fourteenth time?" Those rehearsal "nos" make it more comfortable for me to graduate to the more important ones.

Part of learning to let go is accepting who you are, even when you've let some balls drop. Isa is a dramatic example of this. "I used to be Lisa but I changed my name to Isa. As I was losing weight, and losing my corporate job and losing all the shoulds of where I should be in my life, I dropped the letter out of my name, just like I dropped all those other things." Why don't we try to let an A drop every once in a while just for practice?

Bet Franzone of American Express shared her philosophy of accepting ourselves for who we are: "I think it's important to recognize that you're not going to be great at everything. If you are a wife and you are a mother and you are a star employee, one of those three things has got to give at any given point in the day. I think you need to understand the limitations, choose your battles wisely, and then just keep slugging away."

Another way to let go of doing it all is realizing that you can't... and maybe you shouldn't. Cindy shared this insight. "When I took time off ten years ago, I just wanted to 'catch up.' What I discovered then, and I rediscover every so often now, is that I have to admit that I'll never be caught up; there will always be something more I could do. My father believes that if he ever reaches a point where he has no unfinished projects, if he ever wakes up with literally nothing to do, that'll be it—he'll die. He sees unfinished projects as a good sign—not as something to be overwhelmed by. I am starting to see the value of his perspective.

"One thing I have learned is that there are certain things that I may never get to, no matter how much time I take off," conceded Cindy. "I love photography, for instance, but never find the time to organize my photos into albums. There are some books on my bookshelves that I will probably never read. There are people who I will never really stay in touch with. There are e-mails and voice-mails that will go unanswered."

How to accept that good is good enough? Marsha puts it this way: "One thing I've learned is that life is all about choices and trade-offs. Nothing's perfect . . . and that's okay. Accepting this fact of life has gone a long way toward me accepting myself. I guess I always knew I was a lot of different people, not just the 'president and CEO' identity, but leaving my business has really helped me confirm it. Letting go was impossibly difficult, but I value this time off and highly recommend it to anyone considering it."

Creating a Conscious Career

The one guarantee as you move back into your former job or forward into a new place is that stress and anxiety will still be part of the workplace. If your goal is to lead a life that is both happy *and* prosperous, you will need to take a more conscious approach to what you do next. Relying on old good girl principles of "I'll just work harder" or "I'll make the best of a bad situation" is going backward. This time around, set yourself on having what I call a conscious career, which means paying attention to what you want and evaluating your happiness as well as your performance along the way.

Your first step to a conscious career is to spend some time really thinking about the life and career you want to have. As Type A good girls, it's likely that for most of our lives, we said "yes" to the next job because it offered more money, more status, or more power. But we didn't pause to price out what the job would require—more travel, less free time, overlong days, or a merciless set of demands. After time off, you'll find yourself asking not only, "What do I want to do?" but, "What environment do I want to work in?"; "What kind of culture will allow me to thrive?" and "What trade-offs will I make between money and meaning in my life?"

Debra, who is still sorting out her plans, said, "Over the years, I managed my life around my job. Now I want to manage my job around my life. It's important to set the criteria for what you want out of your life, and then respect your criteria as you evaluate your next steps."

One way to rethink your approach to your work post–time off, is to integrate time off into time on. "Most people define work as going to an office in a full-time job," explained Ardith. "But when I took the time off, I started doing projects for people and realized that *that* could be the new way I worked. My 'time off' became the new way I conducted my life. It provided me with the income that I needed, but it gave me so much more time and freedom to do the other things that I was more personally interested in."

If you choose to return to the corporate world, either in your previous capacity or in something new, choose a position that fits your talents and your passions. Sometimes our first or early jobs relate more to what others, like parents or teachers, planned for us or what we thought might suit us all those years ago. Think of your early career as experimentation, not fate. Ask yourself, not only, "Am I good at this?" but, "Do I love doing this?" Listen for answers that tell you that you are making a difference or that you are uniquely talented at something. Be sure that you wake up excited to go to work.

Getting It Right the Next Time Around

As you make career choices and changes, be as careful about the culture of your company as you are about the content of the job. If flexibility is or will be important to you, be on the look-out for public declarations of corporate policy in these areas. The best companies shout their positive policies from the rooftops. Smaller companies might not have formal programs, but there's an easy way to test the waters. If you ask about examples of flexible arrangements, beware the company that dodges the answer or gives you the hairy eyeball that says, "We don't think that way around here." If you are afraid to even raise the question, that gives you an instant signal that something feels wrong or uncomfortable, and that fear will come back to haunt you.

When you are interviewing with a potential boss, use your best investigative instincts to check out whether he or she is a stress reliever or a stress creator. Does he or she constantly accept inter-ruptions while interviewing you? Does she or he look frazzled, even commiserate with you, "It's insane around here!" Is her office lit-tered with luggage for sudden trips, or bleeping BlackBerries? Worse, is her desk completely clear of any personal photos or fam-ily mementos? Is this the kind of office you envision for yourself? You may be the kind of woman who craves an intense, all-work/no-rest environment, but if not, you are getting an insider's view as to what your life will be like if you say "yes."

Another surefire way to gauge a company's temperature is to start listening as soon as you get in the elevator. Are employees happy, social, buzzing, or are they exchanging their "Oh, I can't believe it's Monday again" horror stories? When I hear employees trashing a boss or a colleague, complaining about the workload, or just looking depressed and sullen, I know that I am entering my per-sonal hell. Corporate cultures change at a snail's pace, if at all. Unless you want to fight like Joan of Arc every day, don't take on a job with the daily battle to change the culture.

The ladies' room is another place for a simple checkup. Not only do women confess quite a few truths about their work life when gossiping behind the stall door, the facility itself is a dead giveaway. Dirty, dark, unsafe, or broken-down bathrooms show you just how you will be treated. If a company can't take care of employees' most personal health needs with dignity, imagine how they will react when you ask to leave early one night for a child's recital?

Check out the company cafeteria. While the dirty, unappetizing cafeteria might seem to be a warning sign, beware the beautiful one with subsidized food. I visited a company recently with a full-blown restaurantlike atmosphere. The hidden message? Get ready to work through lunch and even stay for dinner. You're not leaving your desk for a minute.

Ongoing Regimen for a Conscious Career

If things go well, you will find yourself in a company where the culture is positive, your boss is supportive, and you're doing a good job and working hard. How do you stay aware so that you don't overwork yourself to the stressful brink?

An easy way to create a regular self-analysis is to designate your birthday as your annual checkup. Each year, try to schedule a day or a weekend around your birthday where you spend time alone. Either go away to a hotel for a night, or just "steal" the house for yourself by sending your family away to Grandma's or a local getaway. If you have to go on a business trip near your birthday, arrange to take the next day off and stay in your hotel, work-free but covered for your airfare home.

During that twenty-four- or forty-eight-hour period, plan that you will be in a clean, restful, calm place. Being outside in nature is a great way to open your mind. Build in some treat time, like a massage or a class or a nap, but leave time for yourself to write down how you're doing. You might also include time to set aside for drinks or a meal with some of the people on your "board." Without putting them on the spot with a pop quiz, ask them to give their assessment of what they see going on with you and what they suggest for what's next in your life.

Rather than wait for your annual checkup, you might start to keep track in your journal. Unlike your journal during your time off, think of this journal as your "time-on" record. How are you spending your time? How do you feel about what you're doing? Are you keeping your perspective or are you slipping back into old habits? Let your own voice reinforce the new behavior you are trying to develop.

There are plenty of sources to teach you how to do it, but to get going, it's as simple as getting a nice-looking blank-page book, keeping it next to your bed, and each night or morning putting a pen to paper for just five minutes. Write whatever you want. It doesn't have to be profound or poetic. It just has to be what's on your mind.

The Lake Austin Resort and Spa in Austin, Texas, offers these tips for alternative journals: Create a "discovery book" to record goals, insights, and personal missions. Try making a "collage of creativity," combining drawings and text in a multimedia expression of your inspirations. And a third, think of your journal as a "daily dialogue record" of conversations with yourself, using stream of consciousness about both facts and emotions, by writing continuously for fifteen minutes a day.

Use your "time-on" journal as a reality check on your priorities, preoccupations, passions, and progress.

Just Ask, Again

Today's women are demanding lives that are both successful and personally fulfilling. There is an emerging recognition in the American workplace that flexibility is not an obscenity or an admission of weakness. We can stand up. We can ask. Once you've taken time off, you'll learn that the building won't cave in if we are gone for a few months. If we're as good as our records show, our happiness and longevity with our jobs is the best investment our management can make in their business. Prepare yourself for a conscious career that allows for flexibility throughout the years ahead, one that responds to your continually changing life needs. Your first break need not be your last. The companies in the last chapter prove that the workplace can evolve to support the needs of the humans who work there.

As a final word from the women of *Time Off for Good Behavior*, I asked several of them whether they'd ever do it again. "In a New York minute!" was one of the first responses.

Courtney took her time off seriously. "Time off is an essential luxury. It's not just a vacation. It's taking a break from the 'rat race' you find yourself in, if you are in one," she said. Courtney's time off is just the beginning. "Life is a 'life-long' process of discovering who you are and we are constantly evolving. Goethe said, 'If we do not evolve, we harden,' and it's true. If you don't challenge yourself or desire to make core personality changes for parts that don't work for you anymore, then you'll continue to make the same tragic mistakes," she said thoughtfully.

"Most people can get by 'muddling through life' with their flaws. We all have them, but the truly strong take a hard look at the parts of themselves that hold them back or hurt them ultimately. You have to be willing to go through that hard, muddy space to get to the clearer, freer self."

Lisa K. had this to say about the realities of taking time off: "I would do it all over again, and again and again, but following your passion isn't always easy. You read about women who left their careers, started making jewelry or baking cookies, got on *Oprah*, and lived happily ever after. It doesn't work that way, for most of us (although we all dream about it!). Following your passion means that you still work hard, but your work has more meaning. It's no longer a job, but how you live your life."

Lisa's right. Time off is not a magic formula for happiness or a cure-all for whatever ails you. But it is a step you can take to give yourself the chance to rest and get some fresh perspective to figure out what you need, who you are, and where you're headed next.

"Why did I wait so long?" Donata laughed. "That nagging voice in the back of my head that encouraged me to finally leave the safety of a corporate, every-two-week paycheck in favor of exercising my creativity and raw ambition finally won out (saints be praised!).

Now I am busier than ever, but so much more efficient. I am more challenged, but so much more fulfilled. I am having the time of my life. It's really a question of fear versus fulfillment. Given the opportunity, I would shout from the rafters of every ladies' room and women's gym: 'Girls! Do it now! Don't let fear rule your life. You only have one!' "

And for those good girls still sitting on the fence, perhaps still afraid of taking time off, here's a last bit of perspective from Peggy, who passed on an opportunity to take a company-paid sabbatical when she was thirty-eight. "I know now, fifteen years later, that I am not so indispensable that I couldn't have taken the time off. I also think, although would never have admitted at the time, that I was insecure and that an absence would lead to my company finding out they could do without me. On the contrary, they would have appreciated me more had I taken the sabbatical. You can't go back in time, but I believe had I stepped away I would have achieved the balance in my life that I have now much sooner."

I know that time off changed my life. There isn't a day that goes by that I'm not grateful that I had the nerve to call it quits before it was too late. I am often asked, "Do you ever wish you were back in advertising? Do you miss the big job?" My answer is an unhesitating, "No, not for one minute."

I am happier and healthier, and look at the next phase of my life as another chance to get it right. Taking time off rescued me from myself. You can find your own best life, if you just give yourself some time. After all, you've earned it.

Forging the Path: Cathy's Story

The women in this book had to create their own plans for time off. Their firms had few formal flexibility programs. But the next chapter foretells the future, often thanks to women who were pioneers. First, somebody had to take the risk to step out and ask for it. One of those people was Cathy Kennedy. A twenty-two-year employee of Eli Lilly and Company, she's actually taken two sabbaticals. The second one was company-sponsored. But the first one was of her own design.

"In 1989, I had my first daughter, and at that point in time, Lilly didn't have all the programs it has today," she said. "After coming back to work for nine months, I said, 'This is not the kind of life I want to live or how I want to raise my daughter.' I thought I was going to have to resign because I really wanted to work part-time. Long term, I wanted a career. Short term, I wanted time at home."

Since there was no formal program for flexible time off, Cathy might have packed her bags and headed home. Unlike women who assume that there's no recourse and avoid asking for help, Cathy approached her boss and described her long-term/short-term conundrum. He made her an offer. "We'd like to stay in contact with you," he said. "If you'd like to take three to five years, we'll put you on a leave of absence. We want you to come back to Lilly."

He set her up for a meeting at a Lilly joint venture that needed some part-time help. Cathy worked for the head of Human Resources at the smaller start-up company, three days a week for five years. "If anything, I probably developed more skills because I was in on the ground floor in developing many of their processes. Honestly, it was one of the most rewarding jobs I ever had."

If the concept of continuously working seems to conflict with taking time off, think again about the work ethic of these grown-up good girls. Working hard is second nature. They are no less dedicated or productive. They are just looking for a way to work that can temporarily allow them to deal with the changing nature of their lives.

When Cathy made the decision to move to part-time hours it was agonizing. "I thought I was making a life choice, and it really hurt. It was like admitting that you can't have it all. I felt that I had failed in some regard, that I couldn't do it all. And the fact that I was the first to go on a leave tells you that a lot of other women had stayed on successfully. I looked at myself, thinking, What's wrong with me?"

Again, the standards that highly conscientious women apply to themselves are usually reflective of the very highest performance. Not living up to their own image of success is torturous to them. But because Cathy proved it could be done, the concept of personal leave became a company reality.

"Right after I did it, it became a formal policy," she said. "Today, anyone that has a reason has the ability to take a leave of absence for three years. I'd been back since 1995 and I was in a job again where I was working a significant number of hours. I chose to take another leave for a year, because I have a freshman in high school and a sixth grader, both starting brand-new school systems. I didn't see myself staying home full time. What I'm doing now is working twenty to twenty-five hours a week while the girls are at school, but I can be there before and after school every day."

I wondered if there was a stigma attached to taking off. Cathy said there wasn't. "I was not concerned about it at all."

Cathy's longevity with the company is one indication of her continued loyalty. She's now executive director of Human Resources. In that role, she can set a good example of how taking time off can be part of a satisfying career and she's an effective advocate for the benefits of flexibility programs. "I have total commitment to Lilly. I am absolutely giving one hundred-plus percent and doing a very good job for the organization."

Her advice for women who are struggling with whether to take time off? "I think that you have to follow your own heart and be true to yourself. If I hadn't had the courage to make that tough decision, I might have just stayed with what was appropriate or what seemed like the mainstream. Making that decision has given me confidence in other aspects of my life. Be thoughtful and take accountability for your decision. It might not work out exactly as you planned. Maybe it will turn out better."

Her other advice is to work closely with your manager and to resist the urge to wait till an emotional explosion is ready to hit. She advised, "I didn't go in and say, 'I've got a crisis. I need to be out of here in two weeks because I need to be home.' Instead, I said, 'Over the next several months, I'd like to be in a situation where my work is different. Please work with me on this.' Show you're committed to making it happen."

Cathy also suggests that women look for evidence of a prospective company's flexibility track record. "Today flexibility is so prevalent, that if it's not going on in a company, the question becomes, 'Why not?' "

Calendar Extreme Makeover

Fill in this calendar with a typical week in your life right now, then cross out all of the things that are on your calendar, but are really for someone else.

Time	Monday	Tuesday	Wednesday	Thursday	Friday	Saturday	Sunday
6:00AM							
7:00AM							
8:00AM							
9:00AM							
10:00AM							
11:00AM							
12:00PM							
1:00PM							
2:00PM							
3:00PM							
4:00PM							
5:00PM							
6:00PM							
7:00PM							
8:00PM							
9:00PM							
10:00PM							
11:00PM							
12:00AM							

Time Off for Good Behavior

Fill in this fantasy calendar to represent what a week would look like when you've been granted time off for good behavior.

Time	Monday	Tuesday	Wednesday	Thursday	Friday	Saturday	Sunday
6:00AM							
7:00AM							
8:00AM							
9:00AM							
10:00AM							
11:00AM							
12:00PM							
1:00PM							
2:00PM							
3:00PM							
4:00PM							
5:00PM							
6:00PM							
7:00PM							
8:00PM							
9:00PM							
10:00PM							
11:00PM							
12:00AM							

Look back at the picture of the good girl from Chapter 2. What would she look like if she grew up to live this new calendar life?

Your friends know you well. Ask them how ready you are to consider some time off if you need it. Share your thoughts on a timetable. Are you in crisis mode? Or is it time to make a "someday" plan for a break?

Choose your own board of directors. What does each person offer you? Teach you?

If someone asked you at a cocktail party, "What do you do?" how would you answer? Is that who you really are?

Do you have a story to share? Check out my website, www.time off4goodbehavior.com, for stories from other women who are looking for time off or ready to share what they've learned.

My Mission

The mission of my life will be to (be specific, think big and long term, don't judge or limit yourself): ———————————

———————————————————————————————

———————————————————————————————

In the next year, I'd like to achive (be realistic but aggressive):

———————————————————————————————

———————————————————————————————

———————————————————————————————

Support for Your Mission

I'll Say "Yes" to: (people, events, behavior)	I'll Say "No" to: (people, events, behavior)

CHAPTER EIGHT

A Postscript to America's Companies

Whose fault is it that so many women work so hard that they burn out? From cocktail party chatter to serious media debate, fingers point to America's business leaders as the heartless perpetrators of workaholic stress. Likewise, they are expected to come up with a solution.

It's fair to say that America has overindexed in its unrelenting push for productivity. In an article by Stephanie Armour in *USA Today*, "U.S. Workers Feel Burn of Long Hours, Less Leisure; Employees pay cost of rising productivity," she writes, "U.S. workers put in an average of 1,815 hours in 2002. In major European economies, hours worked ranged from about 1,300 to 1,800 according to the International Labor Organization."[1] So while America can be proud of its productivity, we might take a moment to consider the human sacrifice.

However, in my interviews, women rarely blamed their companies for their own overwrought work styles. To them, corporate America isn't the enemy. Certain jobs may be tough, some cultures may demand 24/7 to earn top dollars, a particular boss might be an ogre, but women indict their own behavior and work styles as the reasons for their escalating stress.

As Lisa B. said, "I don't want to talk poorly about 'corporate America.' It was partly my own doing. When I look back over my twelve-year career, clearly corporate America did not dictate my life. I let it dictate my life."

Good girls, in their pattern of taking responsibility and putting themselves last in line, agree with Lisa, but I believe that companies are accountable, too. If they are interested in retaining the women in their ranks, especially the most talented and valued ones, then it's incumbent on them to take a hard look at their corporate culture and the changing landscape.

The most forward-looking companies are doing just that. If the women in this book had worked for these firms, they might have found a way out of their exhaustion, without heading to the exit. I want to share some of the remarkable and ground-breaking advances of the more enlightened firms in this chapter. They are already seeing the benefits in increased productivity, retention, motivation, and even reduced costs. These companies can serve as role models for addressing the realities of twenty-first-century working life.

The good guys deserve a hand, but the abusers of the corporate workplace also merit some straight talk. So this chapter ends with my advice to the companies whose bad behavior is literally driving their most committed people, men and women, to leave.

Why This Matters

I speak quite often on the subject of being both profession-ally successful and happy. When I preview my story as a good girl who worked too hard before walking out, I get two reactions. The first is a personal one: "Oh, I wish I could do that." The second fol-lows close on its heels: "If you tell that story, everyone will walk straight to their manager's office and quit."

I didn't set out to be the queen of quitting. My goal is to help women take time to take care of themselves so that they can have long and satisfying careers and to help companies understand the truth about what makes their best women tick. Without an honest assessment of the effects of overwork, the problems of burning out the best women will only escalate. The more evolved companies recognize that.

When I was a teenager, there was a poem that we passed around as a way of helping all of us heartsick girls get over a straying boyfriend. The poem, illustrated with a butterfly, read, "If you love something, let it go free. If it doesn't come back, it was never yours. If it comes back, love it forever." Today that poem sounds kind of corny, but in the case of time off, it also rings true.

Companies who create ways to let their best employees go, even for a little while, actually engender more loyalty, as counterintuitive as that may seem. Increased productivity, reduced absenteeism, and a more healthy and motivated workforce are just a few of the reasons that companies ought to open their eyes to the importance of time off.

She's Leaving You

Here are the cold, hard numbers. According to an article by Kathleen Melymuka in *Computerworld,* "a July 2003 survey of 509 U.S. middle managers by Accenture Ltd. found that thirty-eight percent are currently looking for another job and ten percent plan to go job hunting when the economy improves."[2] In other words, many of the women that companies most want to keep already have one foot out the door, or at least a wandering eye on it. The traditional retention strategies are to throw money, titles, bigger offices, or more staff support at the problem. Sometimes that works, sometimes it doesn't. The risk of doing nothing is to lose her and spend money recruiting and training someone new. But if a woman really needs time away, whether to be with children, get a degree, care for a parent, or just climb a mountain, a new solution is called for.

Most of the women in *Time Off for Good Behavior* worked in businesses that didn't offer options. That's why they either quit or came up with their own schemes for time off. A few of the women were lucky enough to work for bosses who were ahead of the curve.

Jane C., a teacher, was able to take advantage of her school's sabbatical policy and meet its requirements for alternative study during her leave. Lalita could have taken advantage of her company's sabbatical program but opted not to, since she knew she wasn't coming back.

Camille, a partner in a publicity business, got her boss's agreement for her leave, and gave her a year's notice so that she didn't jeopardize client relationships or overburden her coworkers. (In fact, now Camille's boss is completing her own leave, lovingly blocked from her computer and voice mail by Camille.) Liz took her company up on their offer of a summer off to regroup, even though her Type A instincts resisted the idea to get paid to chill out.

All were examples of how good girls play by the rules, even when they take a break. But the rest of the women in the book had to make their own way, with no support from their companies, unless it was a severance package.

Innovators of Time Off

Today, dozens of companies are experimenting with inventive programs that give time back to their employees. Many major companies offer paid leaves of absence, including Nike,[3] Charles Schwab,[4] Ralston Purina,[5] Time Inc.,[6] American Century,[7] and Morningstar,[8] as well as many high-tech and legal firms. Many companies offer a variety of unpaid leave, some extended and specifically targeted to help employees wanting to leave and reenter the workforce. Recently Deloitte & Touche LLP unveiled a groundbreaking initiative called the Personal Pursuits program, to allow a period of leaves for up to five years. The key to this program is to keep employees "plugged in" through subsidized training opportunities, a website, mentors, and periodic check-ins.[9] IBM has long offered a three-year program that has reaped retention results.[10]

Flexibility programs are as unique as the companies who offer them. Hallmark, with over one thousand creative people, offers creative renewals, where employees can take largely unpaid time to travel or do photography to keep themselves fresh and inspired. That's in addition to a range of programs, from compressed workweeks and job sharing, as well as paid time off. Overall, most top corporations will try to work with individuals to carve time out for your needs and theirs.

The corporate examples that follow are role models for a new way of working...and living. Their stories reveal a major conceptual shift in the relationship between time off and time on. These companies are willing to take this potentially "threatening" subject out of the closet and put time off into the forefront of a company's culture.

What traits do these companies have in common? All demonstrate that employees' personal needs are at the heart of their company values and mission. They try to create an environment that is flexible enough so that their best people don't have to burn out or leave to get a life. Support for the time-off programs comes from leadership at the very top of the organization. They are good listeners who are willing to experiment and respond to what employees need. And they've embraced a new term for what it's all about: flexibility.

Work/Life Is Over

In the nineties, the phrase "work/life balance" was the catchall for most of the flextime efforts around the country. Ranging from maternity extensions to wellness counseling to day care and parental leave, work/life was really code for "mom and kids," even though programs were sometimes open to dads, too. Some companies added in elder care. But still, the term telegraphed, "moms who need more time at home."

Given that nearly three quarters of women with children under the age of eighteen are working, many moms would say that they have come to terms with the struggles that still accompany child-care needs and a working life. Some days their "system" works; some days it doesn't. But many companies have had over a decade to come up with programs (some better than others) to address women's concerns as moms. While there are still no perfect answers, the mom issue is neither new nor ignored. Self-directed and company-endorsed time off, on the other hand, is a newer concept for companies...and for women. Women's needs aren't isolated to motherhood issues. All women are looking for time for themselves, simply as human beings.

The language of "flexibility" is infiltrating the human resources community. "Flexibility" conveys a work environment that is more responsive to women *and* men, with all different kinds of needs, whether young or older, married or single, parents or not.

Ernst & Young: Flexibility as a Way of Work

Maryella Gockel, Ernst & Young's Flexibility Strategy leader (formerly known as their director of Work/Life Integration), describes flexibility versus work/life this way. "Saying 'work/life' felt like we were trying to separate your work from your life, or that your work wasn't part of your life. We believe that in order to be a great place to work, and an employer of choice, everyone needs to be successful personally and professionally, so 'flexibility' doesn't feel like we are trying to take away from your work to give you your life."

This kind of thinking aligns well with the way that women think about their lives and their work. Integration of work and life are closer to reality. Women acknowledge that it's hard to be happy at work while unhappy at home, and vice versa.

Deborah Holmes is an Ernst & Young partner and the Americas director of the Center for the New Workforce. The nature of the accounting industry was one of the biggest reasons that Ernst &

Young addressed flexibility in a big way. Ernst & Young recognized "the difficulty of combining a very demanding career in a professional service firm, with a life outside of work." Deborah noted that it's particularly an issue at the entry level, when younger women look at the more seasoned women above them to see if there are any role models for flexibility. "It's my belief that the reason so many women need to take leaves is because their workplaces ask too much of them and burn them out. If you pace yourself for the longer haul, you won't need to opt out in order to recoup. Our emphasis is not on providing escape valves, but rather on creating an environment in which escape valves aren't necessary for people."

E&Y has a range of leave and flexible work options, including personal leave, parental leave, leave for elder care and education. But one of the most natural options that makes good economic sense is STOP (Sequential Time Off Program), which takes advantage of slower times, such as the quieter pre-tax-preparation season, to allow employees to receive partial pay while they stop working for short periods.

Diane Doster, tax compliance specialist, has taken a STOP for three years. She's off for three months, but gets paid for one, and she's responsible for her portion of her benefits payments. Diane is the mother of two children who are very active in sports. By taking the slow period off at the end of the calendar year, she is able to attend her children's practices and games and prepare for the holidays, "but not be nearly as stressed as a lot of people. It creates the best of both worlds for me." Come January, she's back at work for tax season, an asset to both her and Ernst & Young.

Wells Fargo: Room for All

With a workforce that's 65 percent female, Wells Fargo is a laboratory for interesting time-off options. Pat Callahan, executive vice president for human resources, said, "We're a company with twenty-four-hour-a-day coverage in a lot of time zones, so there's room for a lot of flexible scheduling and we take advantage of it." Flexible work programs are popular at Wells Fargo; human resources estimates that as many as 30 percent of employees work on flexible schedules. The company allows employees to apply for personal, unpaid leave periods of up to twenty-four months with benefits intact, while employees pay their share of those costs. One program which has been in place for two decades that Pat noted is the Volunteer Leave Program, where "team members can apply for leave of up to four months to work for an organization in their community, such as a local school or nonprofit."

Like Deborah, Pat also sees a new emphasis on flexibility among younger applicants. "I have conversations with our incoming class of college graduates, and flexibility is something both men and women talk about more and more. Some of it's about family, and some of it's about people keeping in shape, or wanting to do more community service. I think that people want to have more in their lives and if you're working twelve hours a day, every day, it's very difficult to have anything else in your life . . . except sleep. Young people are into balance early on, and I think that's not a bad thing."

I've seen that shift in young women as I've traveled to speak on college campuses. In the past, I was asked to talk about leadership and crisis management, and now it's inevitable that no matter what the topic, female students want to know, "How do you get balance in your life?" They are already calculating how or when they might have children while working, if their chosen career path will leave room for a life, or whether the salary rewards will be worth the price of achieving them. They are visibly concerned that the concept of a balanced life is a myth.

At the other end of the age spectrum, Pat notes the effect of too much work on senior women. "It's a problem for anybody who lets themselves get too focused on one thing. Because that career isn't who you are all by itself, and if something happens to that job, it gets very difficult for people to feel their self-worth. I see that more often with senior women than with senior men."

Carrie Knapp, manager of the Corporate HR Project Office, took advantage of Wells Fargo's personal leave program to spend time with her young son. "I realized that he was growing up fast and that soon the idea of spending the summer with his mother would not appeal to him. I had just a precious few years left." But at the time, Carrie was leading a project that could not be abandoned, so she approached her manager and explained that she wanted to spend the following summer with her son. The advance consideration gave all involved time to plan.

"I wasn't paid my salary, but the company maintained their portion of my benefits and guaranteed my job, so there was no worry about coming back to work," Carrie said. What was her leave like? "It was fabulous. I was nothing but a mom for three months. I really enjoy working. I've been doing it for twenty years and I enjoy working for this company. But I had this brief period of freedom where every day my son and I could wake up and do whatever we wanted to do. I'm so happy I had that opportunity because he did grow up and he doesn't want to spend the summer with me anymore," she laughed.

"My best advice is to plan ahead," she said. "What I chose to do was to be honest with my management and work with them so that we could maneuver the project assignments so it wouldn't be burdensome to anyone." The result is that Carrie feels even more loyal to the company, and Wells Fargo retained a valuable and motivated employee.

Eli Lilly and Company: Changing with Women's Lives

Candice Lange, a twenty-seven-year veteran of pharmaceutical giant Eli Lilly and Company, is the director of workforce partnering. She pointed to the subtleties of leave periods that go beyond traditional maternity leave boundaries. "Very talented and motivated individuals find that they need to take a break. They want to be able to give their children a head start into preschool, or sometimes to help them through a difficult adolescence, or be able to work with their elderly parents while their parents were still with them. We have probably between one hundred and one hundred fifty people every year who take advantage of these leaves of between one and three years. About half of them come back to the workforce."

Where some corporate naysayers might respond to Candice, with, "See, I told you so!" she takes a more holistic view. "We work very hard to recruit the best. If we can get half of them to accomplish what they want to get done at home and come back, we think that's a win-win."

One of the hallmarks of the Lilly program is that it's possible to combine elements of the program in ways that suit individuals. She's seen employees move from one flexible program to another to accommodate their changing life needs. Longtime employee Cathy Kennedy's story, in the preceding chapter, showed how she was able to do this. Candice points to her as an example of what most women experience. There are thousands of women like her at Lilly where 88 percent of employees arrange their schedules on flextime and 65 percent telecommute.

At Eli Lilly and Company, a self-directed career attitude is encouraged. Not everyone does this. It's up to you to blaze your own trail and take control and make your voice heard.

Deborah Holmes of Ernst & Young agrees that the responsibility for speaking up belongs right in the lap of individuals. "By 'saying something,' I do not mean approaching someone belligerently, with a chip on your shoulder," says Deborah. "Seek to understand in an open way why these things are happening. Do as good a job on your own behalf as you do on behalf of your boss or your client or your family." In other words, speak up for yourself. It's the only life you have.

Xerox: Responding Over Time

Customized flexibility might be a way to sum up the Xerox program. Paula Fleming, director of Human Resources Effectiveness, described a range of options as different as the women themselves. "I have a woman working for me who has two children. After the birth of the first child, she came back working at an 80 percent schedule, four days a week. Two years later, she had her second, and then continued her 80 percent schedule. She's a valued employee, and we're more than happy to do that. The risk is losing her altogether. She's got a big job, but we've managed to structure it so that it works to her benefit and to ours."

If the goal of companies is to retain talent over a lifetime, then the solution can't be a one-time answer. A second child is born. Someone hits a midlife crisis. Companies can choose to ignore this reality, or respond to it. The Xerox philosophy is to make short-term accommodations for long-term retention.

Paula said, "An HR peer of mine in the UK who had hit a wall said to her manager, 'I need a break. I've got to get out of here and do something completely different. I don't know if I'm going to come back, but I know staying here now isn't working for me.' He worked with her. She took a three-month leave of absence, went off to Australia, did some sailing, some fishing, some lounging around. She came back refreshed and said, 'This is what I want to do, this is where I want to be.' It's been terrific. She just really needed to get away." Paula's comfort with the open-endedness of this kind of leave is an indication of the confidence that Xerox places in their people. As an added comfort, the Xerox personal leaves keep benefits intact for the first ninety-one days.

A big part of Xerox's success with these varied arrangements is training. As Paula says, "We've baked the importance of flexibility into our management trainee programs, to make managers see the need to help people balance their lives. Different people are at different points in their careers, and their personal lives are going to need different kinds of flexibility. We encourage managers to talk about those things."

Leading companies develop a culture that doesn't stigmatize participants, but openly supports applicants for flexibility. Each year, the National Association for Female Executives conducts a survey to assess and select the Top Companies for Executive Women, and it's published in the September (Winter) issue of *NAFE Magazine*. According to NAFE president Betty Spence, the 2003 survey included a new requirement for making the list of honorees. Now it's not only key to have strong programs in place, but to report utilization of the programs. If the "underground culture" makes it a career killer to take time off, the program is meaningless.

Volunteering is a motivation for some who leave. A highlight of Xerox's portfolio of leaves is their social service leave, wherein employees can apply for a three- to twelve-month sabbatical to work on a community cause of their choice. Nancy Scott, sales representative, was granted a leave to volunteer with a local literacy organization. What did she learn? "A successful high-tech organization is a pressure cooker environment, as it should be, but I think I came back with more freshness and perspective. Meeting my sales target is important, but it pales in comparison to issues that pertain to literacy and the cycle of poverty. I came back with an increased sense of self, and that's important."

Accenture: Holding on While Letting Go

In the world of corporate nomenclature, none has a more positive ring than Accenture's program, "Great Place to Work for Women." Pamela Craig is responsible for the U.S. Women's Steering Group, as well as Accenture's senior vice president for Finance. The Great Place for Women program is global. "We try to work in each location around the globe to flexibly provide the options that women need to advance and be successful. To us, flexibility is more important, on the margin, than compensation," says Pamela.

One of the many programs that would answer the cry of so many of the women in this book is the recognition that weekends are being devoured by work, especially by business trips that spill over to Friday or begin on Sunday nights. "We have programs so people can have full weekends at home. If someone is at a client's location for several days running, then they would follow that with several days at their home location."

When employees are on any of their leave programs, Accenture believes that it's important to stay connected to the company. They have three thousand women registered on an online site as "alumnae" and "it's a way for us to stay close. We can provide information about what's going on at Accenture, and it allows the women a way to stay in touch with each other. We post jobs on there when we hear of them.

"Additionally, women who are home to deal with pressing family matters may feel the need for contact. If the length of the leave makes it impossible to guarantee a specific job on return, our concern is that former employees may be forgotten when new hires take their place. Women need on-ramps back into companies, and this is a simple way to keep the conversation going."

Pamela puts responsibility for guidance on the women themselves. "As you're thinking through your own options, explore flexible options for time on or programs for time off. One of the things I have found over the years is that people don't necessarily know about all their options, because they haven't had a reason to." She even advises women to "suggest an option if there isn't one. In Accenture's case, we'd do our best to try to come up with something that works."

Accenture Manager Rebecca Harding had been with the company for six years when she took eight months off to teach English language skills at the Hanoi School of Public Health. "I just wanted to do something exciting and go away to another country as a social service. It clarified for me that I was in the right job. Being in that environment, seeing people live the way they do, put things in perspective. I came back with a much clearer conscience, about what was important to get done today at work versus what's important for me to get done in my life."

That revelation—that life priorities are at least as worthy of attention as job demands—is good medicine for good girls everywhere.

Intel: Scratching the Seven-Year Itch

Spokesperson Gail Dundas described the Intel culture as a place where risk is encouraged, diversity is the norm, but with seventy-eight-thousand employees in forty-five-plus countries, "Any one solution is not going to be the right one. You can't say, 'Okay, everybody can telecommute on Fridays.' " But despite Intel's round-the-clock demands and the predominance of manufacturing schedules, they've developed a portfolio of flexible plans. Telecommuting, compressed work weeks, even employees working wirelessly from Starbucks are acceptable options. Their focus is on results, rather than just hours.

"Our employees' lives today are not clear cut along the lines of what you do in your work versus what you do in your life," said Gail. "So we try to give our employees flexibility so they can meet their commitments, either at work or personally. When they volunteer in the community, they don't have to worry about clocking in."

After seven years, employees take an eight-week sabbatical. They chose the seven-year mark because they were noticing that there was a dip in productivity around the seventh year. "It's not a benefit you've earned because of your service. It's an incentive for continued service. You have to take it all at once. You can add your vacation to it, which is three to four weeks, so ultimately you can have twelve weeks off at once in one year."

What employees do with their sabbaticals is pretty amazing. One engineer tagged ducks for the Alaska Department of Fish and Wildlife. Others have traveled to adopt children. But Lila Ibrahim's story is possibly one of the most remarkable.

Lila's father was raised in an orphanage in Lebanon. "My father was a huge influence in my professional path. I really wanted to thank my father for the sacrifices he made in his life to enable this for me. Also, I was always on the go at work, and needed to take a step back and reconnect with what was important to me. I was going to build a computer lab at my father's orphanage to provide a better education for the kids. I pitched the idea to the Intel Foundation and they said that for every dollar I was able to raise they would match it. I started with a bare room. We did all the rewiring and bought tables and chairs and built a network of twenty-one computers. I taught workshops for the teachers. Basically, no child is turned away." Lila defines good girl.

Lila's project has continued since her sabbatical, with two more computer labs built by her and her friends. Her post-sabbatical feelings? "I'm thrilled to be here at Intel, and I don't think I would have had that kind of opportunity [otherwise]. I'd still be plugging along at work and probably be questioning the same things that a lot of the women reading your book are. Is it worth taking the risk of quitting my job and completely changing my lifestyle? I needed my soul to be refreshed. I feel like I'm a better person having taken the time off, then coming back clearheaded with a sense of purpose and without having given anything up. I chose Intel for the culture, where you work hard, but you are rewarded, not only professionally, but personally."

In listening to Lila, I can hear the voices of so many other women. They love to work hard. They just want to know that at the point in their lives when they need a break, they can take one. The result is not only a happier and more productive employee, but a loyal one, with a sense of purpose in her professional and personal life.

Credit Suisse First Boston: Ahead of the Curve

Imagine taking two months off with your husband and children to spend time together as a family. That's what Kris Klein, managing director of Credit Suisse First Boston did last summer. The four of them followed the Lewis and Clark trail, stayed at a dude ranch, visited friends in New York City, and Kris and her husband were able to take some solo time biking around the San Juan Islands off Seattle. "As opposed to writing or having some ambitious objective, I got to spend the most uninterrupted amount of time I've had with my children since maternity leave." Good for Kris? Yes. Good for the company? Absolutely.

Their sabbatical program has been credited with helping employee retention and contrary to the belief that once free, an employee won't return, Credit Suisse First Boston has experienced a 95 percent return rate after time off. Employees take their first month off at 100 percent pay, the second at 80 percent, and the third at 60 percent of salary.

Alicia Whitaker, CSFB's Global Head of Training and Development, explains how their retention efforts got started. "Starting with the whole tech boom and Internet frenzy, we began losing people to small start-ups and to alternative careers where people thought they'd become zillionaires overnight. The junior people came to us expecting, 'If I'm going to work hard, I don't want to wear a tie, I want to have my dog with me, I want to take more time off, and where's the free Starbucks?' Senior people began leaving for other opportunities outside the industry. We also wanted to attract and keep the best."

The convergence of these needs birthed a slew of programs, introduced under the banner of flexibility, such as a week of honeymoon leave, a compulsory one-month vacation for people who are promoted from analysts to associates, and the sabbatical policy. Alicia explained the rationale. "The context was to make this a better place to work and to recognize that our industry attracts hard drivers who want to do their best and are naturally hardworking, but as they have families, they want to develop other muscles in their emotional repertoire."

Kris is a great example of a hardworking woman. One of the best advantages she experienced by being away, besides the pleasure of being a family, was seeing that her colleagues stepped up to the plate in her absence and accelerated their own development. Kris also felt a professional boost, because, as she said, "a sabbatical gives you a fresh perspective, in the ways you approach business." She's become an internal advocate for the value of sabbaticals.

What Credit Suisse First Boston has learned is that the sabbatical program not only boosts retention, but is a cost saving in the face of alternative of recruiting and training new employees. Angie Casciato, CSFB's Global Head of Diversity and Inclusion, put herself in the shoes of an employee who may be on the fence. "I can leave the firm and take two months off and go somewhere else. But why would I want to leave a firm that I like so much if I could make it work, personally and professionally?" From the company's perspective the cost savings are significant. "When a person leaves, the experience goes out the door, clients potentially go out with them, the revenues would follow, and add to that the average cost of replacing someone. Why not keep someone who's in good standing in the firm? Sabbaticals are important."

Angie's calculations show that companies who care about flexibility are also operating in the best interests of their bottom lines. And the effect of their programs extends to the clients, to the families of their employees, and to the day-to-day company culture that will invite the next generation of hardworking women.

American Express: Hard Work Has its Privileges

American Express sees itself as a values-based organization, rather than a rules-based one. And when employees perform well, there are many options for them to tap for flexibility. "We are creating an environment where people are motivated, where they are encouraged to achieve, where they're empowered and developing over time. We have a core set of behaviors that define what high performance is," said American Express spokeswoman Bet Franzone. In an effort to understand what employees desired from the company, a U.S. survey was conducted and among the top concerns was flexibility. "It was an awakening in some ways," said Bet. "While offered intermittently, flexible programs weren't consistent across the board, so we created the Alternative Work Arrangements Program, allowing telecommuting, working from home, compressed workweeks, and other flexible programs. Now about 29 percent of our workforce takes advantage of this."

Employees with ten years of service can apply for a paid sabbatical of up to six months to work in community service. The program is a reflection of the company's Blue Box values, one of which is to be a good citizen in the communities in which they live and work. "This is a terrific recruitment and retention tool," said Bet. "It's a win-win for everybody. Some volunteer to give back. But there is probably a handful of folks who may be a little burned out, and they get revived and regenerated and a new sense of loyalty."

Employee Relations Manager Suzette Gross, who works in Phoenix, Arizona, took advantage of the program when she worked for a foster care agency in their LifeBooks program. "These are scrapbooks for kids who are in the foster care system, literally a book that captures their lives because so often these kids move from place to place and don't really have a sense of identity." Suzette worked with children to search out their pasts and find photographs of the people and places that made up their lives. "When you go to the ceremony at the end of the program, and present that book to that child, there is no feeling that compares," said Suzette. "One girl didn't expect to receive a book because we had no pictures, but about a week before, we got about two hundred pictures from her foster mom and pulled her book together, the biggest one at the ceremony. She was so touched."

Afterward, Suzette was even more committed to the company. "Three months was a good amount of time to be away," she said.

Suzette was honest with the challenge of taking time away. "The hardest part is to fully disengage. While on sabbatical, there was a hearing that came up regarding a work issue. It was important for me to attend, but I was conflicted about balancing the needs of my employer with my responsibilities at the foster care agency. I did end up going to the hearing." But then Suzette would ask herself, "What if I were hit by a bus . . . if I weren't there, what would happen? I just said to myself, I'm not there. I'm not juggling two jobs. I'm focused on this sabbatical. That was healthy for me."

Bet also expressed a need for honesty in the workplace. "As women, we need to recognize our limitations. It's worth having an open discussion about any issue you may face, how your work life may be affecting your personal life or vice versa. Unless you engage in that discussion, people are just going to figure that you have it all together because that's the aura you put out."

General Mills: Women to the Rescue

One of the ways that enlightened companies come up with programs that answer women's needs for flexibility is to ask their own women what they want. Seven years ago, when Lydia Mallet joined General Mills as vice president and chief diversity officer, she started a process that put gender on the agenda. She invited senior women to meet and articulate their concerns and fears in order to create a community. Lydia pointed to why the formal process was necessary. "So often women collude by not saying anything. They seem to have the belief 'If I don't ever talk about being a woman, then nobody will notice that I am one.' It's not necessarily conscious, but it's a way to survive."

As a result of this open communication, the company put in place a number of flexible options, from adoption or paternity leave, to childcare resources and referral systems, as well as flextime, part-time, and telecommuting. Now almost half the employees use flex work arrangements, with unpaid leaves available for those who need them. These programs are open to men and women, and benefit both, but with many of the companies, women were the first to voice the need.

Lydia described their philosophy about time off. "It's not that we're hoping every employee takes a leave, but I think that anybody who had the courage and assertiveness to say, 'I'm an excellent performer, and I don't want to leave the company permanently, but I need a break. Can you accommodate me?'—we try and work that out."

The story of General Mills' Maria Jenson concludes this chapter.

That's what happens when companies exercise good behavior. What advice do I have for those who don't?

A Word to Business Behaving Badly

How can more companies get it right? One place to start is to look at the stories just told. Perhaps their best practices can be adapted to fit your industry. If you're looking for more inspiration from more companies who do well by their women employees, consider these sources: *Working Mother* magazine publishes an annual survey, "100 Best Companies for Working Mothers," featuring corporate profiles grouped by sector, broken down into data on Advancing Women, Childcare, Flexibility, Leave for New Parents, and Work/Life.

The National Association of Female Executives tracks the "Top 30 Companies for Executive Women" each year in *NAFE Magazine.* Here you can learn about the level of female participation and leadership in various companies and about the features the editors especially like about each.

Catalyst, the nonprofit research and advisory organization, dedicated to advancing women in business, also annually adds to their substantial knowledge about women in the workplace. Each year, the coveted Catalyst Award honors several companies for their innovation in recruitment, development and advancement of managerial women, and the presence of female board directors. You can find more information, and honorees dating back to the 1980s, at http://www.catalystwomen.org.

Repairing bad behavior starts with facing the truth of the insidious expansion of the 24/7 work life. Whether you blame the lengthening and intensifying work calendar on the tough competitive times we live in, the tightening economy, or on technology's ability to leash us to our job around the clock, the result is the same. Today's employees are working longer and longer hours and taking less and less time off every year. Their stress doesn't come from just the hours they put in, but from their acute level of personal responsibility for the job and their inborn urge to overwork.

Many women say that they check e-mail the minute they awaken. They listen to voicemails on the way to the office, punch into their cell phones for phone meetings at every corner. I have heard countless stories of women afraid to go on vacation without their computers. Monitoring e-mail is a way of life at the beach, so as not to miss something critical or at least to prevent postvacation e-mail avalanches. Some women told me that they are expected to dial in to conference call meetings while on vacations, or even fly back to the office during time off.

The occasional high-pressure work spikes are normal, but this high-test everyday style is eating away at the ability of women to even get a night's sleep, let alone have a life. While some women brag, "I'm too busy to take time off," most will secretly admit that they are starved for a break. College graduates look at companies with an eye toward balance from the start. Young moms slam face-first into the reality of living two lives, where neither a crying baby nor a demanding boss show mercy. Your most seasoned workers, women in their forties and fifties, ask, "Why am I still running like this?"

Being over our heads with being busy has become a badge of honor. It's also a warning of impending burnout. Quantity of hours worked seems to supersede quality of results achieved.

In a *BusinessWeek* cover story, reporter Diane Brady wrote

about Ann Fudge, the CEO of global ad agency Young and Rubicam.[11] At age forty-six, at the top of a superstar career, Ann took a two-year sabbatical to spend time with her family, but mostly to spend time with herself. While interviewing Ann's colleagues and peers for the article, Diane heard many comments, like that from one unnamed senior executive, who said, "I just don't know if someone who can spend months on a bicycle has the 24/7 drive we need." In other words, the only way to show dedication to work is to never, ever stop. In a career that could span forty to fifty years, that's a frightening life sentence for professional success.

As a manager of a business, it's not unfair for you to expect your people to put in their time to earn extra rewards and promotions. But your measure of employee contribution ought to value quality of output, rather than simple quantity of hours worked. The changing lives of women in this century, and of men, as well, demand new ways of measuring commitment and performance. Can the new determinant of dedication be results, rather than face time? Can you begin to let go of the model that the hardest workers are necessarily those who show up earliest and leave latest? (If it takes that long to complete their work, are they truly efficient or are they overtasked or wasting time?) Can you stop saluting your most loyal employees as only those who will drop vacation plans with family at a moment's notice? The quantity-versus-quality measure of productivity is long overdue.

She's Right Before Your Eyes

Often your best people are the ones that are cheerfully burning out right before your eyes. After one corporate speech, a manager came up to me and said, "I'm worried about Sarah. She's just what you described. She's an incredible worker, but I think she's really burning the candle at both ends. I guess I should talk with her about that." Later, I spent time with Sarah, a mom of two, and she was nearly in tears. "They keep changing my goals, making it impossible for me to do all this at the same time. I am beginning to lose it." Would the manager have ever been comfortable having a conversation about how Sarah's *doing*, instead of just how much she's producing?

One company I spoke to expressed concern about the satisfaction among their best women, and I said, "Well, when you do performance appraisals, do you spend any time asking them how they are instead of telling them what they did?" "Oh yes," said one of the senior managers there, "we always do that." One of her staffers overheard our conversation, and as she walked me to the door, she whispered, "They never ask anything about how we're doing." And if they did, would women tell them the truth?

As someone who once managed hundreds of people, I know that I couldn't deal with a mass exodus of employees heading out for time off. But just as we are willing to reward our best-performing employees with bonuses and other perks, why can't we open our minds to the idea that time is the most valuable reward in our time-starved, stressed-out world?

Attitude Adjustment

How can business adopt some good behavior? My first advice is to make an attitude adjustment toward the people who ask you for some time off. Some managers may feel annoyed with the young women who talk about balance and life issues during the job interview process. Bosses get frustrated with young moms who want to extend their maternity leaves, or ask for additional time-off periods during the growing years. Others are flabbergasted when a star forty-year-old decides she needs to find herself. And corporations may be insensitive to the needs for time and self-assessment among the fifty-plus women who are considering whether they should spend their final fifteen or more working years developing their companies or rescuing their personal lives. Your irritation with these brave employees will spread like wildfire and convince others that you don't really want to hear what's on their minds.

Feeling mystified, annoyed, or frustrated is natural. But open-minded listening is a better response. Unfortunately women, especially the good girls, don't make your job any easier because they tend to keep their problems to themselves, solve it on their own (or fail to) and come to you when it's too late.

Publicizing your programs, getting the word out that your company isn't shut down to options, is important. Encouraging networks within the company where women can exchange their ideas for a better workplace is another avenue. Consider establishing valuable mentoring programs where senior employees, male and female, connect with women on the way up. Usually, those dialogues are about how to get ahead. It might be equally interesting to include conversation and counseling about work/life issues so that women can be coached to deal with the strain of a hard-working life and to relieve it before it gets out of hand. Share the stories of those who leave and return so that others will see that it can be done.

As you seek to develop your own flexibility practices, the company stories just told should be a starting point. Their innovations and lessons learned can be adapted to fit your industries.

Creating a Livable Workplace

Maybe developing programs like the ones cited in this chapter seems too ambitious. Here's an easy start. Can you mandate that your employees take the vacation they are granted? Can you request that there are no cell phone calls to the office, no e-mails while they are off? Can you train your managers to stop asking employees to call in over the weekend or participate in long-distance meetings while on personal time? Can you encourage your people to use their weekends to rest?

Set an example yourself. Don't suppress your own stories of relaxing vacations or fun leisure activities. Tell employees about the movie you went to or the restaurant you tried. Let them know you enjoy a personal life, too.

There have been projections that taking time off will someday be part of the American culture. Right now, it seems a distant hope. I have joked that I was featured in the national press as a maverick for taking five weeks off. If I lived in Europe, I'd be considered a workaholic who didn't take all her allotted vacation. We are a hard-working country that's proud of overwork. But the costs of piling our demands for near-workaholism onto the work ethic of the good girl are clear.

Addressing the issues of time off for good behavior can benefit all employees, women and men. Just as the voices of moms have challenged the policies and benefits in the U.S., and created options for dads, too, the pioneers of time off are paving the way for all of us to enjoy successful careers and happy lives. How like the good girls to take care of everyone else, too.

The Next Generation: Maria's Story

The future of flexibility could be personified by Maria Jenson, Marketing Director for Pillsbury Frozen Products, General Mills.

Maria's career is an example of what flexible work may look like in the coming years, but she was also a pioneer before flexibility was more common at General Mills. "In 1994, when I was a pregnant assistant marketing manager who already had two kids, there were not a lot of positive examples of balance and flexibility. I feel lucky to have ridden the wave of increased options. I made each request for flexibility with some anxiety, but each time General Mills has been willing to work with me."

Maria took a six-month leave after her third son was born and then came back part-time. "There were very few 'part-time' jobs at that time so the only real option was fitting a full-time job in fewer hours," she said, "but I was so pleased to have the option that I worked an eighty to ninety percent schedule for over two years." In fact, she was promoted while on her part-time assignment. She then took an international assignment in the UK. While there, she was asked if she were willing to be considered for two big assignments in the U.S., but she deferred so that her eldest son could finish school in the UK. "With my sons spread through lower, middle, and upper schools, a husband with his own hectic career, and the frustrations of fighting London traffic, there were times I bordered on meltdown. That provided the motivation for the whole family to take a year's leave."

She decided that she wanted to spend a year "reveling in our family of five, before becoming just four, with my oldest son college-bound. Looking back on that year, it seems like a huge gift filled with wonderful memories. We caravanned through Europe and jour-neyed through Asia, Australia, and New Zealand. We homeschooled the two younger boys, having designed much of the curriculum around the countries we were traveling to. We saw and learned so much and experienced many world events up close. We were in Bali during the bomb, Malaysia during the war, and China during SARS. We all have a much broader view of the world and a much greater appreciation for home."

When she returned to work, she found that she was even more committed to the company. "Because I had the time to consider dif-ferent options, I better understand why I made the choice to work at General Mills. I also spent a whole year reconnecting with my kids and husband and so felt less conflicted regarding work. Refreshed, reenergized, and recommitted . . . not a bad deal for a year off with no pay."

As companies consider the risk of letting women go out for a break, they should also anticipate the resulting loyalty that a break engenders. "I feel that the company values me and they are willing to think about my career as a long-term proposition," said Maria. She's realistic about what she's given up in exchange for flexibility. "Though I recognize that some of the choices that I have made, like part-time work and leaves, have slowed down my career progression, I feel that I was in control of those choices. I have always felt I had to 'reprove' myself after each variation from the norm, but I have not felt punished or sidelined for those choices."

Now Maria is back in Minneapolis working for the Pillsbury division. As she looks back on what she learned, she offers this advice: "I wish I had realized earlier that life is not a sprint. Nor is my career. The hardest part of taking a leave from work is believing that in the scheme of a thirty-plus-year career, that a break will not have a negative impact. Each situation is different and each person will have to evaluate the risks, but if a leave of absence will be the break you need to be able to keep working, then it's a clear win. Even if the motivation is rest, reflection, or reconnections, the rewards are probably greater than the risks, for both you and your employer."

Company Checkup: How Flexible Are You?

On a scale of one to ten, ten being excellent, how would you rank your company relative to the flexibility issues raised in this book?

_____

If you listened in on a private conversation among a cross-section of females in your organization, how would they grade you?

_____

Does your company have a formal or informal network for women? Do the flexibility issues come up? _____

_____

What's the biggest barrier keeping your company from trying some of the best practices in Chapter 8? _____

_____

Which women in your company do you see facing these issues most? Younger prospects? Moms? Forty-plus women?_____

_____

What's the biggest cost to you of women who leave/are stressed-out? (Retention? Absenteeism? Customer service center depletion?)

_____

_____

_____

Who's the person in your organization best suited to lead a forum on these issues? _____

What three things could your company implement immediately to address flexibility?

1. ———————————————
2. ———————————————
3. ———————————————

What three things wouldn't cost the company anything? What could your company give up (early meetings, always-on e-mail access) that would aid the issue?

1. ———————————————
2. ———————————————
3. ———————————————

How can you differentiate from your competitors by being the most flexible employer, especially in a high-tension/high-stakes category?

————————————————————————
————————————————————————
————————————————————————
————————————————————————
————————————————————————

EPILOGUE
THE WOMEN OF <u>TIME OFF FOR GOOD BEHAVIOR</u>—"AFTER"

As you read these parting thoughts from the women featured in *Time Off for Good Behavior*, realize that while many have moved on to more exciting ventures, achievement is not the new A in their lives that they're most proud of. It's the way they feel and live their lives that's the true beauty of taking time off.

Eileen, fifty-five, married, mother of a sixteen-year-old, is named executive director of the American Montessori Society, a lifelong dream job. "I learned that I love to network...if I could be paid to look for a job, I would."

Lisa K., thirty-five, married, two children, age seven and three, managing partner of Artemis Woman in Vermont, dedicated to empowering women with wellness-inspired products, "Women have a very strong voice inside. Listen to that voice."

Peggy, fifty-three, married, president of nonprofit advertising organization in New York, never took time off. "I could have been a little nicer to myself and nurtured myself more, but I have no regrets."

Monique, forty-three, married, twelve-year-old daughter, owner of three bed-and-breakfasts and an author, lives in Brooklyn. "A lot of people stay in their lives because it looks good to other people... the bottom line is that you have to make time for you."

Donna D., forty-four, married, is now a life coach, with a fourteen-year-old son, "who needs me more now than when he was six!" On her life now: "Security is the power to do whatever I need to do."

Lisa B., thirty-seven, single, consulting in real estate and travel, now in Boynton Beach, Florida, "I will never, ever allow myself again to feel like I have no way out."

Courtney, thirty-four, divorced, working but searching for her next calling. "I don't feel like I have to be the worrying expert every five seconds of my life."

Ann, forty-seven, married, three daughters, abandoned her plan to take the sabbatical for the time being, given her financial and career priorities. "I know I made the right decision and I also know my time for more of me will come."

Rosemary, forty-one, newly married and now a board member of her former childcare company in Boston. "What I want to do is take this year and put myself in circumstances that will touch my heart."

Camille, forty-four, married, two children, age ten and thirteen, returned as president of her literary public relations firm after five months with her family in Rome. "The American ethic of work, save, work, save . . . and then you're sixty-five and then you can travel . . . what makes you think you're going to be able to do that?"

Kerry, thirty-three, married in Vermont with her nine-month-old baby boy, entrepreneur/designer of a company called the Better Boob Job, www.thebetterboobjob.com. "People said I was crazy, but I'm selling in boutiques across the country."

Donata, forty-two, married, nineteen-year-old stepson, four-year-old son, founder/creative director of Donata LLC, a company that celebrates life at home. "When we take a step into the unknown, that's when the truth comes to pass . . . and we end up happier."

Bonnie, fifty-one, married, business strategist and motivational speaker, now lives in St. Petersburg, Florida. "None of us are paid enough that we are that important that the world stops if we're not around."

Lalita, fifty-five, engaged, author of bestseller *Cane River*, lives in Silicon Valley, California. "I'm not sure I'd have the courage to repeat my actions of nine years ago, but the resulting life change worked for me emotionally, spiritually, and financially, and I'll always be grateful for that."

Debra, forty-six, married, an eight-year-old son and four-year-old twin boy and girl, in the process of figuring out her next move while getting her life back, in Westchester, New York. "I sleep like a baby ... talk to me in six months when I'm no longer the former anything."

Isa, thirty-five, single, body awareness expert and teacher/owner of dance studio Temple of Poi in San Francisco. "I'm so much happier, the only thing that is the same is my determination."

Ardith, forty-three, has added a four-year-old black Lab named Cleo to life with Dave. She's a marketing consultant, singer, and jewelry maker in Santa Fe. "I finally feel that I have that elusive 'work/life balance.'"

Joan, fifty, married mother of a fifteen-year-old daughter, back in her hometown of New York after a year in Paris and in the process of defining her next move. "I am aggressively looking but not worried, because I will not dishonor my very important year."

Diana, fifty, married, with a twenty-one-year-old daughter in college and a son entering high school, business owner in Boston, Massachusetts, and hasn't taken time off. "I wish there were a way to get that long-term success without the heavy personal sacrifice I've had to pay, but I'm not willing to let that goal go."

Julie, thirty-six, returned to the same Washington, D.C., firm, refreshed from a year spent in the Far East. "My intuition is sharper and that has surprising effects in business meetings. I would do it again in a heartbeat."

Peri, forty-five, married, two daughters, media executive for a major retailer, living in Elgin, Illinois. "I've always said that I have an office and a home. Those are two different things."

Liz, age forty-six, single, is the second sister of *The Satellite Sisters*, a syndicated radio talk show and website, as well as an author, a marketer, and a philanthropist. "Know yourself...you need to be switched on."

Pam, thirty-nine, single, is now an independent marketing consultant in New York. "It's not only important to like what you do, but to find the right environment to do it in."

Kay's now forty-six, she's at home with her children, age five and a half and seven, and has created an interactive knitting website, www.masondixonknitting.com. "I get to do two things I love, write and mentor people."

Diane, fifty-nine, single, nonprofit president in New York City and Hudson, New York. "I don't think you can ever get rid of Type A, but you can decide where your Type A-ness is focused."

Donna G. forty-four, single, senior VP of consumer products in sports marketing. "I wish I had some time to take time off...I work too much!"

Karen J., fifty-two, married with a high school-age daughter she stayed home to raise, now working heavy part-time as an executive at a new creative service company. "People asked me if I missed working, but I know being a mom is work."

Leslie, forty-seven, married, two children (a twenty-year-old son and a month-old daughter), president of a boutique recruiting firm in New York City. "I am now once again starting this journey and have arranged for a scaled-back work life with my newly adopted daughter."

Jane C. is now forty-seven and daughter Katie is now ten; Jane returned to her teaching job having learned that "the most important thing is that you love your life."

Cindy, forty-three, single, president of her own consulting company and author of *Work Naked*. "I'm finally listening to that small voice inside that gets muted by other people's voices."

Jane B., fifty-five, single in a long-term relationship, human resources consultant and coach for women. "Had I known it would take so long to make my new career pay off, I might not have taken the leave...but ignorance was bliss and I really have no regrets."

Marsha, fifty-five, married with three adult sons, in Montclair,

New Jersey, now an advisor to businesses, a cantor, composer, performer, independent scholar and lecturer on classical and Jewish music. "If there is something that you have a burning desire to do, don't expect that life is going to serve you up longevity."

Marilyn, fifty-eight and married, with two adult children, has created an entirely new career as an author and expert in the decorative arts. "If you have the financial resources, go for it."

Catherine, fifty-two, started her own brand consulting company, but made the move without taking time off between jobs. "I've probably given too much of myself to work and looking back could have taken more care of myself."

Karen N., fifty-seven, married, two daughters, age seventeen and thirty-five, owner of a fashion lifestyle company, living in Ross, California. "When you create a business that has emotion attached to it, it can be around for a long time."

Terry, forty-five, moved to Charlotte, North Carolina, to be CEO of a nonprofit organization and just got married, her wedding "was a blast."

Barbara, forty-two, mother of three children under ten, ran a triathlon in Texas while telecommuting for her New York public relations firm. "There's always going to be somebody else to put first. For you own sake, you need to say, 'No, I need this for me.'"

And Mary Lou, fifty, celebrated her twenty-fifth wedding anniversary with Joe, founded a women's marketing consultancy Just Ask a Woman, wrote a book called *Just Ask a Woman*, and became a motivational speaker who "strives to be the person my dog thinks I am."

NOTES

INTRODUCTION

1. Hope Dlugozima, James Scott, and David Sharp, *Six Months Off: How to Plan, Negotiate and Take the Break You Need without Burning Bridges or Going Broke* (New York: Henry Holt & Co., 1996):, 2.

2. Stephanie Armour, "U.S. Workers Feel Burn of Long Hours, Less Leisure: Employees pay cost of rising productivity," *USA Today* (final edition, December 17, 2003): B01;http://proquest. umi.com (accessed January 13, 2004).

3. Ibid.

4. American Institute of Stress website, "Job Stress," http://www. stress. org/job.htm (accessed April 15, 2004).

5. Pamela Paul, "Time Out," *American Demographics* (June 2002): v. 24, i. 6; 34 http://search.epnet.com (accessed January 12, 2004).

6. Neal Learner, "Labor Shortage Ahead? The *Christian Science Monitor* (January 6, 2003): 16. http://proquest.umi.com (accessed June 2, 2004).

7. Judy Greenwald, "Few companies preparing for impending labor shortage; Work/life programs can ease pain of crisis," *Business Insurance* (October 27, 2003); 10, http://www.nexis.com (accessed January 9, 2004).

CHAPTER TWO

1. Paul J. Rosch, M.D., "Type A Behavior: What You Should Know"; http://www.msnbc.com/onair/nbc/nightlynews/stress/default.asp (accessed January 20, 2004).

2.   Ibid.

3.   Ibid.

4.   Waino W. Suojanen, et al., "The Emergence of the Type E Woman," *Business* Abstract (January–March 1987): v. 37, n. 1; 3(5) http://web7. infotrac.galegroup.com (accessed January 20, 2004).

5.   George L. Fleming, "Does Birth Order Dictate Behavior?" *Knight Ridder/Tribune Business News* (March 24, 1997): p 324, B1262; http://web1.infotrac.galegroup.com (accessed January 16, 2004).

6.   Rita Koselka, Carrie Shook, "Born to Rebel? Or Born to Conserve?" *Forbes* (March 10, 1997): v. 159, n. 5; 146(4) http://web1.infotrac.gale-group.com (accessed January 16 2004).

7.   Ibid.

8.   Joanne Cleaver, "A Crummy Situation: Despite workplace gains, women still aren't making the dough that men are," *Chicago Tribune* (November 5, 2003); 1, http://proquest.umi.com (accessed January 16, 2004).

9.   Debra L. Nelson, Ronald J. Burke, "Women Executives: Health, Stress, and Success," *The Academy of Management Executive* (May 2000): v. 14, ii, 107, http://web 1.infotrac.galegroup.com (accessed January 16, 2004).

10. Ibid.

CHAPTER THREE

1.   Catherine Arnst, "Women Work, the Support System Doesn't," *BusinessWeek*, 00077135 (November 4, 2002): 13806; http://web1. epnet.com (accessed January 16, 2004).

2.   Nelson, Burke, "Women Executives."

3.   Ibid.

4.   "Female Executives Seek Top Jobs," *Association Management* (October 2003): v. 55, i. 10, 24(1), article A108970274; http:// web1.infotrac. galegroup.com (accessed January 16, 2004).

5.   Sylvia Gearing, "If I'm Such a Success, Why Do I Feel This Way?" *Executive Female* (November–December 1995): v. 18, n. 6, 46(5) http://web7.infotrac.galegroup.com (accessed Jan 20, 2004).

6.   "How Do I Know If I'm a Workaholic?" www.workaholics-anonymous.org (accessed April 29, 2004).

7.   Sue Shellenbarger, "Multitasking Makes You Stupid: Studies Show Pitfalls of Doing Too Much at Once," *The Wall Street Journal* (Eastern

edition, February 27, 2003): D1: http://proquest.umi.com (accessed June 1, 2004).

8.   Ibid.

CHAPTER FOUR

1   Haidee E. Allerton, "Not Funny Ha Ha, Funny Peculiar," *T & D* (December 2003) v. 57, i. 12; http://web1.epnet.com (accessed January 12, 2004).

2.   Jennifer Schramm, "Time Squeeze," *HR Magazine* (August 2003): v. 48, i. 8; 128 http://web.1epnet.com (accessed January 12, 2004).

3.   John de Graaf, ed., *Take Back Your Time: Fighting Overwork and Time Poverty in America* (San Francisco: Berrett-Koehler Publishers, Inc., 2003): 205.

4.   Ibid.: 26.

5.   Diane E. Lewis, "Survey Forecasts Focus on Recruitment," *Boston Globe* (January 4, 2004): G.2; http://proquest.umi.com (accessed January 13, 2004).

6.   Cleaver, "A Crummy Situation."

7.   Sharon Epperson, "A Woman's Web: Money doesn't distinguish between the sexes, but there are women's sites worth a visit," *Time* (November 27, 2000): v. 156, i. 22, 100; http://web5.infotrac. gale-group.com (accessed May 31, 2004).

CHAPTER FIVE

1.   Jennifer Merritt, "Why Women MBAs 'Stop Out'; Sharon Hoffman of Stanford's B-school says they feel safe in suspending their careers and tending to home because the degree cushions the risk," *BusinessWeek Online* (November 21, 2002); http://web7.infotrac.galegroup.com (accessed January 23, 2004).

2.   Carol Krucoff, "De-Stress Yourself: Regular Exercise Helps Maintain Health Under Pressure," The *Washington Post* (July 6, 1993); z.12, http://proquest.umi.com (accessed April 21, 2004).

3.   Ibid.

CHAPTER SIX

1.   James Lardner, Trena Johnson,"World-class Workaholics," *U.S. News & World Report* (December 20, 1999): v. 127, i. 24; 42 http://web7.info-trac.galegroup.com (accessed January 20, 2004).

2.   Claudia Wallis, "The Case for Staying Home," *Time* (March 22, 2004): v. 163, n. 12, p. 52.

3.   Kristin Rowe-Finkbeiner, "Juggling Career and Home: Albright, O'Connor and You," *Mothering* Magazine (March 1, 2003): 28.

4.   Ibid.

5.   Center for Women's Business Research, press release, "Capturing the Impact: Women-Owned Businesses in the United States"; http://www.nfwbo.org/pressreleases/nationalstatetrends/capturingtheimpact.htm (accessed May 31, 2004).

6.   Lynnley Browning, "A Burnout Cure That Few Companies Prescribe," *The New York Times* (July 6, 2003); 3.7 http://proquest.umi.com (accessed January 13, 2004).

7.   De Graaf, *Take Back Your Time*, p 25.

8.   Sue Shellenbarger, "Work & Family: One Legacy You Don't Want to Pass on to Your Children—Workaholism," *The Wall Street Journal* (January 15, 2004): p D1.

CHAPTER SEVEN

1.   Fay Hansen, "Truth and Myths About Work/Life Balance," *Workforce* (December 2002): v. 81, i. 13; http://web3.epnet.com (accessed January 23, 2004).

2.   Wallis, "The Case for Staying Home": 53.

3   Barbara Sher, *I Could Do Anything If I Only Knew What It Was: How to Discover What You Really Want and How to Get It*, (New York: Delacorte Press, 1994): 33.

CHAPTER EIGHT

1   Stephanie Armour, "U.S. Workers Feel Burn of Long Hours, Less Leisure," B01.

2.   Kathleen Melymuka, "Already Gone: A brain drain is coming when the economy improves, and your top IT talent may be headed out the door," *Computerworld* (December 8, 2003): v. 37, i. 49, 47; http://web2infotrac.galegroup.com (accessed June 2, 2004).

3.   Browning, "A Burnout Cure."

4.   Ibid.

5.   Samuel Greengard, "It's About Time," *Industry Week* (February 7, 2000): v. 249, i.3; http://web7.epnet.com (accessed January 16, 2004).

6.   Browning, "A Burnout Cure," 37.

7.   Ibid.

8.   Toddi Gutner, "The Pause that Refreshes," *BusinessWeek* (November 19, 2001): i. 3758n, 138, http://web17.epnet.com (accessed January 12, 2004).

9.   Anne Marie Chaker, "Luring Moms Back to Work; To Fight Female Fight, Some Companies Overhaul Leave Programs; a Five-Year Break," *The Wall Street Journal* (December 30, 2003): D1; http://proquest. umi.com (accessed January 13, 2004).

10. Ibid.

11. Diane Brady, "Act Two: Ann Fudge's two-year break from work changed her life. Will those lessons help her fix Young & Rubicam?" *BusinessWeek* (March 29, 2004): 72.